The Seven A̶   ̶?

Pro   ..a McLean
Mary Riddell
Dr. John Coleman
Lord Ralf Dahrendorf
Helen Wilkinson
Frank Field MP
Harry Cayton

Edited by
JOHN LOTHERINGTON

CENTRE FOR REFORM

London

Published in March 2002 by:
Centre for Reform
Dean Bradley House, 52 Horseferry Road
London SW1P 2AF
United Kingdom

Tel: 020 7222 5121
Fax: 020 7222 5185
E-mail: info@cfr.org.uk
Website: www.cfr.org.uk

ISBN 1-902622-31-6
ISSN 1463-6751

Printed by
Contract Printing,
1 St. James Road,
St. James Industrial Estate,
Corby, Northants. NN18 8AL.
United Kingdom

CONTENTS

Notes on Contributors

Harry Cayton is Chief Executive of the Alzheimer's Society. He serves on a number of statutory and voluntary bodies including the Central Research & Development committee of the NHS, the public involvement committee of the Human Genetics Commission and the NHS Modernisation Board. He publishes and lectures on health, social policy and ethics. He writes here in a personal capacity.

Dr John Coleman trained as a clinical psychologist and worked for 14 years as a Senior Lecturer in the Department of Psychiatry in the Royal London Hospital. Since 1988 he has been the Director of the Trust for the Study of Adolescence, an independent research and training organisation based in Brighton. He has published a number of books, including *The Nature of Adolescence*, now in its third edition. He is a Fellow of the British Psychological Society. He was awarded an OBE in 2001 for services to youth justice.

Lord Ralf Dahrendorf is a social scientist, the author or editor of over forty books, and a Liberal Democrat member of the House of Lords. Following a distinguished academic and political career in Germany, he joined the European Commission in 1970. Moving to the UK in 1974, he was director of the LSE from then until 1984, and Warden of St Antony's College, Oxford from 1987 to 1997, where he also served as Pro-Vice-Chancellor of the university from 1991 to 1997.

Frank Field MP is Chairman of the Pensions Reform Group. He was Director of the Child Poverty Action Group and Director of the Low Pay Unit before he was elected Labour MP for Birkenhead in 1979. He was a front bench spokesman on education and social security, and then Chairman of the Social Security Select Committee. Following the Labour election victory in 1997, he served as Minister for Welfare Reform in the Department of Social Security until 1998.

John Lotherington is Director of the 21ˢᵗ Century Trust, an NGO based in London which promotes the exchange of ideas among younger leaders worldwide on the issues in international relations and public policy which are likely to be the main challenges they will face in the coming decades. He writes here in a personal capacity.

Professor Sheila McLean is the first holder of the International Bar Association Chair of Law and Ethics in Medicine at Glasgow University and is Director of the Institute of Law and Ethics in Medicine at Glasgow University. She has acted as a consultant to the World Health Organisation and the Council of Europe, and is regularly consulted by the media on matters of medical law and ethics. She has published extensively in the area of medical law and is on the editorial board of a number of national and international journals.

Mary Riddell is a weekly columnist for *The Observer* and an interviewer for the *New Statesman* and the *Daily Mail*. She is a former deputy editor of *Today* and has written for *The Guardian*, *The Times* and *The Daily Telegraph*. Her writing awards include Interviewer of the Year in the British Press Awards.

Helen Wilkinson is the Director of Genderquake, a strategic consultancy focussed on the gender dynamics of social, economic and technological change with a non-profit and member based arm, www.Genderquake.com. She is a regular contributor to newspapers and magazines and frequently quoted commentator. She has written widely on relationships and family policy. As one of the pioneering members of Demos, she now sits on its Advisory Council.

Foreword

Standard Life is pleased to have sponsored 'The Seven Ages of Life' project.

As the largest mutual life assurance company in Europe, we are committed to providing customers with a wide range of financial products and services which meet their needs in an ever changing society. We are keen to support work which encourages individuals, organisations and government to reflect upon the issues which affect people as they move through life. This book does so in an engaging and stimulating way.

I am grateful to the editor and authors for their contributions to the seminars held in Autumn 2001 and for writing their chapters.

Scott Bell
Group Managing Director
March 2002

Introduction

John Lotherington

In one way Margaret Thatcher was right when she claimed that there was no such thing as society. It is not simply one lump, although neither is it the case that it can be reduced solely to individuals and families. People belong to many different groups, and they and their inter-relationships can be viewed from different perspectives - class, culture, creed, and in this case, following Shakespeare but not too closely, those defining points in the life-cycle which are the Seven Ages of Life.

This collection was the brainchild of Nick South, who would have been the editor had his career not taken him abroad. The conception, developed further by Anthony Rowlands, Director of the Centre for Reform, was to place in sequence discussions of the most pressing issues pertaining to different stages in the life-cycle. The contributors are all distinguished by their close involvement in these issues, but they come from diverse professional backgrounds, including politics, academe, think-tanks, NGOs and journalism. They are not from one single political tradition and they follow no set agenda. Except when stated otherwise, they are writing here in a personal capacity.

The contributors tested their ideas at a series of seminars organised by the Centre for Reform in the autumn of 2001. It became clear that there are emerging issues portrayed here by the contributors which are not yet fully confronted in the political arena, and old problems which persist but are neglected in comparison with immediate crises in the public services. The aim, therefore, is to redress the imbalance in public debate.

Complex choices ushered in by new technologies, poverty both in old and new forms, and the re-formulation of values are three themes which run through this collection. Discussing birth, Professor Sheila McLean guides us through what was once seen as an event, albeit not a simple one, but is now becoming a series of choices. With ever developing possibilities of medical intervention, there is controversy surrounding the rights of the foetus and the impact of those on the rights of the mother. Genetic science is forcing us to re-think the boundary between natural and unnatural, what is permissible and what not. As Professor McLean points out, we are facing the re-politicization of private decisions.

Mary Riddell illuminates the condition of childhood and challenges the often distorted perception of it through adult eyes, whether in panic about child murderers, as in the Jamie Bulger case, or at another extreme in unrealistic visions of the innocence of childhood. She asks the thought-provoking question: what is childhood for? Parents seem less sure and yet more conscious all the time of the risks associated with it. Having explored the wider context to the Damilola Taylor case, she reminds us that the experience of childhood is not uniform and that government is in danger of neglecting the priority of eradicating child poverty.

Dr John Coleman examines the transition into adulthood and also emphasises the economic conditions which can make that precarious. Changes in the labour market have seen the elimination of many of the traditional opportunities for young people, only partly remedied by expanded access to further education. Sexual activity is one way young people assert adult independence, and this gives rise to a range of concerns, such as sexual health and teenage pregnancy. He stresses gender difference in the transition to adulthood and the vulnerabilities this involves; in particular young men are thought about, all too often, only as a threat to society. He calls for 'joined up' government to become more of a reality in policy-making with regard to young people, and greater sensitivity to their changing circumstances, especially in changes to the structure of the family.

Helen Wilkinson looks at these changing structures as she charts the rise of the 'liberal family'. With the increase in the divorce rate and, even more markedly in recent years, the trend towards cohabitation as opposed to marriage, the traditional family is on the wane. However, the needs answered by family life (when working well) remain, the family being the basic unit of society, a network of support and the foundation of emotional well-being. While seeking to preserve freedom of choice as far as possible, Helen Wilkinson argues that the law should recognise the new shapes that family life has taken and ensure that appropriate rights and responsibilities are upheld even outside the traditional bounds of marriage.

Lord Ralf Dahrendorf discusses a work society running out of work as traditionally defined, along with the technological changes which have brought us into the 'knowledge society' and its division between new 'hi-tech' work and old 'high-touch' work. He highlights the dangers for those marginalised or relegated to insecure and unsatisfying 'high-touch' work, as capital becomes less and less dependent on labour and vice-versa. He explores how this affects the 'realm of freedom' and argues that freedom - activity that is autonomous, self-determined action - should become increasingly a feature of work, contrary to Marx's assumption that freedom and work must remain mutually exclusive.

Frank Field returns to the theme of poverty as it dogs people in retirement. He makes the case for tackling that poverty through a Universal Protected Pension, a compulsory, funded second pension on top of the basic state pension as it exists at present. He points out the urgency of this, given the demographic increase in the proportion of retired people in the coming generations. Securing sufficient income for nearly all retired people to live independently of state support is, for him, the prerequisite both to enjoy those expanding opportunities for activity open to older people and to face up to those problems which accrue later in life.

Harry Cayton brings us to the close of our seven ages, with reflections on how our perceptions of dying have changed in the context of increasing secularisation and following two world wars, the Holocaust and the advent of AIDS. He shows how the medicalisation of death has transformed our experience of it, and he takes us full circle to the new complexities of choice accompanying new medical capabilities. He discusses how people can exercise choice about the care they are given when dying, and advances a compromise with regard to euthanasia, arguing not for its legalisation but that mercy-killing should be a defence against a charge of murder, much as is self-defence.

Taken together these essays have important implications for broader issues in public policy. The general reflections on these which follow are mine, and do not necessarily represent the views of any of the individual contributors or the Centre for Reform.

A recurrent theme in this collection of essays is freedom. That is, freedom which needs to be interpreted in the conditions of the 21st century, where the old unacceptable limits to its exercise still exist but where also choice, open to us and forced on us, is becoming more complex and becoming so at a dizzying speed. That complexity increases with medical technologies, which give the possibility of so much greater control over how people come to be and how their lives draw to a close. From childhood through to retirement, the communications revolution and the dynamic of global capitalism give new choices (some would say fake choices) in information, alternative world views and material goods, which re-shape the divisions in societies along generational lines as well as between those who have access to these new choices and those who do not. Old solidarities, in nation or neighbourhood, class or creed, are under strain; it was within these old solidarities that certain freedoms were upheld, others denied, and the distinction between liberty and licence seemed obvious, rightly or wrongly. Where autonomy can begin and end now seems to become ever fuzzier in each of the stages of life. This requires a thoughtful, continually adaptable liberal response in policy-making, as an alternative to both a reactionary stance and the top-down approach of the present government.

There are those who cling to verities which served in previous generations. The Right in recent years has been muted in creative political debate, preoccupied by Europe while persisting in the battle against socialism despite its demise. As the tide of complex choice and social change rises, much of the vigour of public debate will depend on whether modernisers on the Right will renew their conception of autonomy or, Canute-like, just seek to defend past limits and understandings.

The collapse of the policy on soft drugs proposed in 2000 by Ann Widdecombe, then Shadow Home Secretary, illustrates the failure to appreciate changes through the stages of life, and its effect on the more general political debate. The press knew it had a field day ahead of it when the policy was announced of tightening up the criminalisation of cannabis smokers. Given the widespread practice or toleration of cannabis smoking among the young, up to those now in their 40's, a number of the younger Tory MP's were bound to have indulged, and, one after another, members of the shadow cabinet in early middle age were forced to line up and confess. The significance of this fiasco was that it is only in its aftermath that the Labour government has felt able to begin the up-dating of drugs policy to correspond to changing values. In areas of social change and expanding choice, the politically dominant progressive force in British politics is in thrall to conservative anxieties.

For New Labour this hesitation in social policy is, of course, a consequence of electoral arithmetic. With the decline of the old industrial economy, the traditional working class basis of support for Labour also declined, famously making it crucial that Middle England be brought on side and kept there. Middle England, its vision of the future clouded by a sensationalist press, tends to react adversely when it comes to new, possibly threatening choices, or changing values, or the persistence of problems among those who now lack a political voice. There is, therefore, little political reward for New Labour in promoting public debate about many of the hard choices which affect us in various ways in the seven ages of life. As a consequence the Third Way can often appear little more than re-heated, one nation conservatism with an updated marketing gloss.

In theory there is more to the Third Way than that. Thinkers such as Anthony Giddens have shown how political thinking needs to be re-orientated away from class and towards globalisation. In this post-industrial age the working class has vanished in terms of theory, just as it has been marginalised electorally. However, while class politics once obscured other divisions in society, so the emphasis now on economic positioning in the world obscures some of the complexities which people face at different points in their lives. Education is a key case study of this.

Before the NHS came to dominate the headlines, education, education, education was the central concern and remains so in the guiding philosophy of the Third Way. Only through effective education can people flourish in a globalised economy, which places the highest added value on the manipulation of information, and can face the challenges of the risk society where old job security is dead and where all individuals need to be equipped to change life-paths as the world changes around them.

But how well have educational policy-makers and schools responded to the old and new challenges posed in the seven ages of life? In terms of curriculum content there is a continuing, creative response. Biology teachers introduce their students to genetic science and the novel choices it offers surrounding birth; personal and social education as well as pastoral care offers young people guidance as they negotiate their way across the changed terrain from childhood to adulthood, and, notwithstanding the absurdity of Section 28, they are alerted to some of the decisions they will need to make in forming and sustaining relationships as they become independent; an ever increasing emphasis on IT fits them for a world of work where bytes not widgets are what will matter; religious education provides a forum where many cross-cutting ethical issues are raised, including, of course, those concerned with dying and how modern medicine is transforming that. However, beyond these features of the curriculum, there are clear limits to education's capacity to respond to the concerns highlighted in this collection of essays, just as there are limits to the effectiveness of educational reform.

A command and control educational system, operated from Whitehall through aggressive, costly inspection and rigid targets, leads to distortions and Soviet-style 'storming the plan' to deliver whatever is specified while neglecting anything less tangible. There is demoralisation among those at the chalk-face - or the keyboard. An over-loaded and over-traditional National Curriculum denies teachers the creative space to respond to changes in the world around them as they are specific to the children and young people in their care. The emphasis on new technologies is concerned very much more with skills than with the understanding of how technology is transforming our world, or the increasingly complex choices it will offer individuals as they grow up and as adults in their work and leisure. Faced with declining solidarities, citizenship is added to the curriculum, but alarmed by the post-modern world (as well as rightly concerned with equal treatment of different faiths), encouragement is given anew to faith schools, in place of any fundamental review of how all schools sustain and are sustained by their communities. The link between poverty and educational failure is denied; but while schools in deprived areas should not be defeatist, child poverty is still one of the most significant indicators of educational outcomes, and, for the student, debt and economic insecurity loom ever larger. Those whose educational outcomes are bad are often alienated and more prone to crime and/or low status, insecure jobs in the service economy; unadapted to new technologies, they are the bad risk in risk societies.

Following school and college, lifelong learning is gradually becoming a reality in connection with re-training and leisure skills; this is essential to address the growing division between 'hi-tech' and 'high-touch' workers discussed by Ralf Dahrendorf. But there is also lifelong learning to be done in connection with technologically transformed matters of life and death, and that is a gap left to be filled by over-worked GPs as best they can and by a press generally at its worst. There needs to be a transformation in social attitudes to adult learning. It is still seen by many as in most respects remedial, addressing past failures in childhood and youth, rather than learning being integral to all stages of life. And, while economic imperatives must be clearly acknowledged, an emphasis in lifelong learning should be about learning as an end in itself, about access to the good life for individuals, as well as the continual adaptation of the work-force to new conditions.

Education is being geared up, albeit with grinding slowness, to meet the challenges of a globalised world, but it is not systematically concerned with freedom in its changing forms or the old obstacles to it. And one way it should be audited, as begun here, is to measure it against the concerns inherent in the seven ages of life. A liberal policy would need to ensure that professionals in education, along with appropriate input from students and parents, had the freedom and the resources to respond creatively to those concerns, and to ensure that that policy was developed in the context of a broad interpretation of lifelong learning and of a social policy truly joined-up to guarantee opportunity for all.

Another area of government policy which has a very direct effect on the concerns raised in this collection is poverty reduction. The end to poverty is seen not simply in the supply of material wants but in inclusion in society, specifically through work and taking on the risks and responsibilities - and freedoms - of financial independence. But this means not allowing people to opt out in the drive from welfare to work. The problem then is that the pressures brought to bear on the unemployed chip away at freedom from a different direction than the financial, and even financial freedom through work may be very limited when the minimum wage is set at so low a level. There is also the problem of poverty among those who cannot work and are necessarily dependent, the young and the old. The attention focused on child poverty is yielding only slow results, but that poverty is crushing in its effects and clearly demands a more rapid increase in resources devoted to its elimination. For the old, makeshift social security arrangements are in place, but half-hearted pension reforms give little hope for the future - reform no doubt being half-hearted because the political pain would have to be borne now while the benefits would only unfold in successive generations.

These problems of poverty are not just ones that persist, they too are changing. As wealth increases and its symbols change, so does relative poverty. Children may be socially excluded - denied those opportunities their peers take for granted - even though their basic needs are met. Poverty in old age is not merely a constant problem but threatens to grow dramatically in scale. The proportion of old people is growing as the birth rate shrinks and people live longer; private provision for retirement can cope with that only in part, and makeshift social security will come under terrific pressure. So the solution to the problem of poverty may stay beyond our reach without some radical re-thinking. And, in formulating policy, it is vital that those with little or no political voice - the young, the old, the poor - are not merely the objects of social management but have their concerns and freedoms taken fully into account.

Viewing such issues through the prism of globalisation may well be vital if Britain is to flourish in a changing and competitive world. However, freedom resides in particular conditions as well as in general prosperity, or indeed in general liberties, and the changes and complexities of that freedom therefore also need to be viewed, as here, through other prisms, such as the seven ages of life.

Birth

Professor Sheila McLean

It is true to say that birth marks perhaps the most momentous step in the life cycle of the human being. On live birth an individual becomes admitted to the world's legal family, and in most - but not all - philosophies acquires the full range of moral human rights. For example, utilitarians such as Jonathon Glover, would not hold that babies necessarily have the same rights as adults. In his reasoning, it is necessary to be a right holder that you also have interests. Babies, he would say, may have biological needs, such as feeding, but they do not and cannot have interests. Therefore, they do not have rights.[1]

However, most people would be reluctant to accept this account of what it is to be a right holder, not least because of the implications of adopting such a view for others in the community, such as those who are suffering dementia or those who are in a coma. It can, therefore, safely be concluded that live birth provides at least the recognition of legal rights to the child, and for most it generates the attribution of moral rights also. As will be seen below, the capacity to claim to be a legal person is highly significant in one's progress through life.

In the first part of this discussion, attention will be focussed on the effect of the acquisition of legal rights on the child him or herself. However, in subsequent parts of the chapter, it will also be necessary to expand the discussion beyond birth as an event and to consider birth as a process. The capacities of modern medicine have served to focus much of the interest in this area on the process rather than simply on the event. Thus, issues arise about who can become pregnant, what kinds of children should be born and the extent to which it makes sense to talk of reproductive choice. These are relevant to the moment of birth as they have implications, as will be seen, which serve in some cases to move reproduction (and therefore birth) beyond the purely private and into the public sphere. The consequences of this will be clearly seen as the discussion progresses but, in broad terms, translation from private to public generally validates increased interventionism; what might be called a re-politicisation of private decisions.

Legal rights and birth

However, this is not to say that the fact of birth, and its associated status, are simple phenomena. The very act of being born is a time of critical importance for the child, and a time at which it is acutely vulnerable. A number of children are born every year with, for example, cerebral palsy, which is thought in some cases to be the result of an incident occurring during the birth process. Equally, some children are born suffering from damage which occurred pre-natally, and still others are born after parents have attempted to ensure that they will have no further children. Each of these incidents can, and very often does, result in legal action in pursuit of compensation for harm caused.

The acquisition of legal rights is what provides the child with the status to raise such an action. In the case of cerebral palsy, for example, litigation may result in the award of substantial sums of damages, which are calculated to restore the child to the situation it would have been in but for the harm caused by the negligence of another. As this calculation includes loss of potential earnings, for example, cases such as this often result in the largest damages awards being made. Although few, if any, would object to such sums being made available, the child's right to sue has implications for the resources available to the health service by deflecting funding from health care provision into compensation. It may also have an impact on the management of birth. Thus in the case of *Whitehouse* v *Jordan,*[2] damage suffered by a child was attributed by the parents to the doctor having pulled too long and too hard on the forceps during delivery. Here, the question was whether or not the doctor's behaviour amounted to negligence. In the event, the doctor was held not to have been negligent and no damages were awarded. But, had the opposite been concluded, both the courts and the doctors feared that an award of damages, following an attribution of negligence, would have had a major impact on clinical freedom.

Children may also - on live birth - sue for damage sustained pre-natally. This right is achieved in England and Wales as a result of legislation[3] and in Scotland by common law.[4] Acceptance that it was possible to litigate for harm which temporally occurred when the claimant was not a legal person followed the reports of the Law Commission[5] and the Scottish Law Commission[6] in the aftermath of the thalidomide tragedy. The possibility that substances ingested by a pregnant woman could mis-shape the developing embryo or foetus had substantially gone unrecognised until that time. When the Royal Commission on Civil Liability and Compensation for Personal Injury (Pearson Commission)[7] reported in 1978, they confirmed that there were known to be a number of substances which could mis-shape an embryo, and many more which might do so if taken in combination with other substances or drugs.[8]

Faced with the undoubted harm which had occurred to some 400 children in the UK and many more throughout the world, the companies involved in marketing thalidomide nonetheless denied their responsibility, even though the drug had been specifically targeted at pregnant women. Only a lively and robust media campaign eventually resulted in damages being paid, albeit without an admission of responsibility.[9] Naturally, a media campaign, while securing some assistance for the children concerned, was unable to resolve the fundamental legal issue as to whether or not a right to sue did, in fact, exist in these circumstances. For this reason, the Law Commissions were invited to consider and report on this question.

The Law Commission's view was essentially that such a right might exist, but for the avoidance of doubt it recommended legislation, a recommendation which was subsequently given effect to by the passing of the Congenital Disabilities (Civil Liability) Act 1976. The Scottish Law Commission, on the other hand, was persuaded that an application of a civil law proposition would suffice, namely that a right should exist where it was clearly in someone's interest that it should. It, therefore, eschewed the legislative route, content that the application of this principle could clearly be extended to children in this situation.

Finally, on the litigation question, some children are born following an attempt by their parents to avoid birth, by, for example, the termination of a pregnancy or the sterilisation of one party to the relationship or the use of other contraceptives.[10] The actions which may follow from this scenario are two-fold. First, the parents may raise an action in what is called wrongful birth[11] and second, the child may attempt to raise an action in what is called wrongful life.[12] Unsurprisingly, neither of these actions is uncontroversial. In the case of wrongful birth actions, the litigation is raised by the parents who had sought to avoid a pregnancy and birth, claiming compensation for the pain and suffering of labour and childbirth. It has for some time been accepted not only that such actions are competent, but also that the damages awarded may include compensation for the additional costs of raising a child. This latter assumption, however, was recently overturned in the case of *MacFarlane v Tayside Health Authority*,[13] which eventually reached the House of Lords.[14]

Wrongful life actions are raised when the child him or herself seeks to obtain compensation for the fact of birth itself. These will generally only arise when the child is born suffering from some disability, unlike wrongful birth actions which can arise whether or not the child is disabled. Although wrongful life actions have occasionally been successful in other jurisdictions,[15] they seem to be precluded by the 1976 Act in England and Wales[16] and have not been considered by the Scottish Courts, although it seems likely that they would not be deemed competent in Scotland either. The reason for reaching this conclusion is substantially that the arguments used to preclude their availability rest largely on public policy grounds which are unlikely to be geographically distinct between the two jurisdictions.

This brief introduction to some of the legal consequences of live birth would not be complete without reference to the fact that amongst the human rights which become available on live birth are the obligations assumed by states, in terms for example of education and health care, which derive from the United Nations Declaration on the Rights of the Child, and other international agreements. Prominent amongst these rights is the right not to be discriminated against on any grounds. Specifically, the Convention on the Rights of the Child says:

'States Parties shall respect and ensure the rights set forth in the present Convention to each child within their jurisdiction without discrimination of any kind, irrespective of the child's or his parent's or legal guardian's race, colour, sex, language, religion, political or other opinion, national, ethnic or social origin, property, disability, birth or other status.'[17]

Interests and birth

Birth has also taken on an added significance for some of the estimated 10-15% of the population who are infertile for whatever reason.[18] Medicine's capacity to circumvent infertility has given hope to many who would otherwise have been forced to remain childless. It is generally agreed that the interest which people have in reproduction is both profound and significant. Robert Edwards, a pioneer in assisted reproduction, has said that, 'The desire to have children must be among the most basic of human instincts and denying it can lead to considerable psychological and social difficulties.'[19]

Nobody seriously doubts the value ascribed to the capacity to reproduce - to give birth to a child. In the previous section, attention was generally focussed directly on the rights which birth bestows on a child. In this section, however, we can clearly see a move away from a sole focus on the child (although arguably birth itself is of primary interest to the child given that without it he/she would have no life at all) towards the recognition and accommodation of the interests of third parties - namely parents and potential parents. It may, at the outset of this section, be worth commenting on the terms of this heading itself. It will be noted that what is being discussed is 'interests' rather than 'rights'. This is a point of more weight than the merely semantic. Although those who have difficulty in conceiving or who are infertile may wish to claim that they have a *right* to assistance in attaining the desire to procreate, which Edwards has so eloquently described as a basic human instinct, it is clear that no such right exists *in se*. The struggle for reproductive rights, which in its modern form was probably begun by feminists in the late 19th century, conclusively shows that, although there may be a negative right not to have existing reproductive capacities removed or interfered with, there is no right as such to be given assistance in reproducing.[20] Nonetheless, over the early part of last century the law ultimately moved away from vindicating and facilitating the intrusion of the state into reproductive choice by way, for example, of restricting access to contraception and abortion and the imposition of non-consensual sterilisations on those thought unfit to parent,[21] towards recognition of what might be called a negative reproductive right. In these terms, reproductive rights essentially focus on the capacity to utilise capacities already in existence (such as fertility) but do not mandate state assistance where such capacities are lacking, as a result of medical, social or psychological causes.[22] The claims of the infertile to a right to assistance in reproduction are, therefore, weak.

However, other more positive rights may attach to reproductive choice and the possibility of conception and birth. Most notably, this can be evidenced by the application of anti-discrimination clauses to be found in many national laws, as well as in international agreements. Thus, equality of access may be anticipated once a service is made available; but the institution of the service itself may not be demanded.

Although the development of assisted reproductive technologies (ARTs) has given hope to many who would otherwise have been doomed to childlessness, the techniques and technologies or ART are not uncontroversial, even some 21 years after the birth of the first so-called 'test-tube baby'. The earliest form of circumvention of infertility, where the fertility problem lay with the male partner, was artificial insemination using donor sperm (DI). Although now widely practised, in the early stages DI was a thoroughly controversial technique, albeit a relatively simple one. For example, it was held in a least one case that the use of donor sperm could amount to adultery in that the woman had surrendered her reproductive capacities to a man who was not part of the marriage.[23] Although this view is now discredited, adultery was one of the matrimonial offences which could have resulted in divorce. Equally, the child born as a result of DI was uncontrovertibly illegitimate, encouraging, it is believed, the falsification of birth records which is, of course, a criminal offence. Since the status of illegitimacy has by and large lost its stigma, this is now no longer regarded as being problematic. In any event, our law now imports a presumption of legitimacy where the male partner has given his consent to the DI, and this is also true in in vitro fertilisation (IVF).[24] The sole remaining controversy surrounding

DI relates to the anonymity of sperm donors. In the United Kingdom, children born as a result of DI are not entitled to obtain identifying information about the sperm donor,[25] although this prohibition has been relaxed in other countries[26] and is currently under debate in the UK.

More controversial, but only relatively so, is the practice of creating babies using surrogacy. Surrogacy may be full or partial. In full surrogacy, the child carried by the woman (who intends to give it up to the 'commissioning couple') will generally be the genetic child of the commissioning couple. Full surrogacy, therefore, can be used when a woman is fertile (as is her partner) but she is unable to carry the child to term. Partial surrogacy exists when the surrogate mother has a genetic link to the child which may also be genetically related to the intending father. This is not the place to discuss surrogacy in depth; it is mentioned to point to the fact that birth - which in the past clearly attributed a certain status, and imported a set of assumptions about parentage - can no longer be taken to do so. Medicine has the capacity, therefore, to create unusual family networks, which has posed a challenge both to the law and to ethics.

An example of this can also be found in the case of *R* v *Human Fertilisation and Embryology Authority, ex parte Blood.*[27] In this well-known case, Diane Blood sought permission from the Human Fertilisation and Embryology Authority (HFEA) to use sperm which had been collected from her unconscious, dying husband. There were a number of complexities to this case, which ultimately led the Government to commission a review of the consent provisions of the 1990 Act.[28]

For the purposes of this discussion, the critical issue was the fact that the sperm had been stored without the written consent of Mr Blood, and that its use was also countenanced without his written consent, both consents being required by law.[29] The HFEA initially refused to permit Mrs Blood to use the sperm, and also refused to permit its export to another country using the export provisions contained in s 24 (4) of the Act. In the event, the Court of Appeal considered that the HFEA had not paid adequate attention to the terms of European Law in its deliberations, and asked the HFEA to reconsider its decision. Although it could arguably have restated its original position, the HFEA ultimately permitted Mrs Blood to remove the sperm to Belgium for treatment, where, happily, she conceived and is now the mother of a son.

There was considerable public support for Mrs Blood,[30] even although using the sperm in this way created an unusual family situation. Of course, it is the case that some children are inevitably born after the death of a parent, but - until modern medicine intervened - both parents were required to be present at conception, if not at birth. In other words, it was a misfortune to lose one parent during the course of the pregnancy, but not an intention. In Mrs Blood's case, however, the intention was to create a child both conceived and born after the death of its father. Both the Report of the Committee of Inquiry into Human Fertilisation and Embryology (Warnock Report)[31] and the then Government[32] had expressed distaste for the deliberate creation of what can loosely be called a posthumous pregnancy. However, the 1990 Act clearly countenanced this situation by creating in s.28 the status of a fatherless child. Although this was probably designed to deal primarily with conceptions arising in single and lesbian women, it clearly also applied to the situation of Mrs Blood. Thus modern medical techniques have enabled the creation not of a child who is unfortunate enough to have a father who died after its conception (but who would nonetheless be the father for legal purposes) but a child whose father was dead before he/she was even conceived, rendering him/her legally fatherless.

Clearly, there are status issues here worthy of concern. First, the very notion of being fatherless might have psychological implications for the child, who will have no father registered on his/her birth certificate. For that reason, and in line with a plausible interpretation of the UN Convention on the Rights of the Child,[33] the final report on the consent provisions of the 1990 Act recommended that children born in such situations should be able to register their biological father as their father on the birth certificate.[34] In 2001, legislation designed to implement this recommendation was talked out in the UK Parliament.[35]

A second implication of posthumous pregnancies is that the child, who would otherwise have inherited from its biological father so long as it was *en ventre sa mere* at the time of the father's death, has no inheritance rights. Thus, a possible financial penalty is paid. Although sympathetic to this problem, the report on the consent provisions of the 1990 Act concluded that inheritance laws should not be changed to accommodate this situation,[36] although it was suggested[37] that specific attention should be paid to who may use sperm in these circumstances, so that *de facto* if not *de jure* the child will benefit from the father's estate.

An engineered birth?

It is not only unusual family units which modern medicine can create. It also has the capacity to permit selection of children themselves, by means of pre-natal screening or pre-implantation genetic diagnosis. Intending parents, therefore, are apparently given additional choices about which embryo to implant (based on its having 'desirable' genetic characteristics) or whether to continue with a pregnancy where some defect has been detected in the developing embryo/foetus. Having said that, the reality of this apparent choice may be tenuous. The British Medical Association, for example, says, 'women's accounts of prenatal screening suggest that they have little real choice in the matter and find it difficult to decline a test that has been offered.'[38]

Strangely, perhaps, pre-natal screening for defects or disorders is a widely accepted, apparently uncontroversial service offered to virtually every pregnant woman in the United Kingdom. I say 'strangely' here because the public seems equally to be in a moral panic about the notion of so-called designer babies, yet in a sense this is what the screening services have long facilitated, albeit in a negative rather than a positive form. It is, for example, the anticipated outcome of a 'bad' screening result that the woman will choose to terminate a pregnancy. Indeed, those who have religious or other objections to abortion will often refuse to undertake the test. Of course, abortion is not an inevitable consequence of discovering that a woman has an affected pregnancy; some families may wish to be screened in order to prepare themselves for dealing in life with a child suffering from a particular condition. However, the link between a 'bad' result and pregnancy termination remains reasonably strong. As the BMA has said:

'In the past, some health professionals restricted access to prenatal diagnosis to those individuals who planned to terminate an affected pregnancy. Although this approach is now widely regarded as paternalistic and unacceptable, a 1993 survey of obstetricians found that one-third still generally required an undertaking to terminate an affected pregnancy before proceeding with prenatal diagnosis.'[39]

As has already been said, then, prenatal screening programmes do have an element of design in them, in that those who are deemed to be 'defective' or damaged will often, whether by choice or as the result of indirect pressure, be screened out of the population by means of pregnancy termination. At the other end of the scale, the desires of some families to select embryos for implantation is often subject to a semi-hysterical public response. Yet arguably the events are not dissimilar in that certain undesirable characteristics are being avoided by choice. In fact, it is arguably the case that selection of embryos for implantation is less morally weighty than the decision to terminate an established pregnancy, but the latter seems to receive less opprobrium (when done on medical grounds) than the former.

Perhaps one reason for this is the fact that the selection of embryos may be sought on grounds which are non-medical. There is, for example, little outcry about selecting embryos where it is intended that only embryos which will not suffer from a particular medical condition will be implanted. Where, however, people seek to choose other characteristics, such as gender[40], then they are likely to be treated with opprobrium. Equally, where embryos are selected in order that they may assist an already existing child by making available compatible DNA, this has also traditionally been met with considerable concern.[41] In fact, of course, it is quite plausible to argue that these choices are no less ethical than those which lead to the termination of a pregnancy. The mere fact that it is social rather than medical characteristics which are being sought does not *in se* render the decision unethical.

And, of course, many seem to fear the possibility of the deliberate creation of children engineered to be taller, more athletic, more intelligent, more beautiful or more in possession of other characteristics thought to be desirable. This, it is said, both commodifies the child and gives them an 'unfair' advantage over others. Two things can be said in response to these arguments. First, on the commodification point, it is not self-evident that parents who seek to enhance their child's chances in this way are commodifying the child. We all seek to enhance the opportunities for our children by, for example, sending them to the best schools or dressing them so that their attractiveness is maximised. This we do not routinely regard as commodification. On the second point about unfair advantages, of course, the same argument can apply.

Some may also fear that the ability to select children in this way will, if permissible in law, be the province of only some members of society, namely the rich and/or the educated. Children born without the 'benefit' of being engineered would then be doubly disadvantaged and their parents' reproductive choices marginalised. This is the scenario played out in the film *GATTACA*. Interestingly the film's conclusion is a triumph for the genetically disadvantaged individual. Such fears, however, are for the moment at least of little practical content, though, should aggressive selection in pregnancy become a clinical and legal reality, they may become a matter of real concern. For this reason, it is important that the ethical debate precedes the clinical or legal reality. Naturally, the arguments in this area are more complex, but this issue is raised to demonstrate a somewhat schizophrenic approach to selection of children.

Birth as a battlefield?

From what has gone before it can be seen that pregnancy and birth are increasingly medicalised. Inadvertently or not, modern medicine has generated a variety of situations in which nature is not simply allowed to take her course. This, it must be said, is the central aim of medicine in all of its forms. The development of antibiotics has saved many lives which 'nature' would have taken. The circumvention of infertility has equally allowed more births for those who would otherwise have been unable to have children. Both of these are deliberate attacks on nature, and few would suggest that what is 'natural' is, therefore, necessarily 'good'. However, the implications of the apparent increase in medicalisation of pregnancies has other consequences which are highly controversial.

One of the many advances in the management of pregnancy has been the capacity to screen the embryo/foetus before birth, as has already been discussed. But screening has also had one further consequence which is even more ambiguous than the consequences already highlighted. The capacity to visualise the foetus in the womb has led, in some cases, to doctors believing that in treating a pregnant woman they are in fact treating not one, but two patients. Thus, although the foetus has no legal rights, pressure may be applied to the pregnant woman to act in ways which are directly for the benefit of the embryo/foetus. This may relate to behaviour during pregnancy or behaviour at the point of birth.

This capacity has contributed to the development of what has been called 'maternal/foetal conflict'.[42] Pregnancy and birth become arenas in which the woman and her foetus are pitted against each other in a battle for supremacy. Arguably, this has resulted in increased policing of pregnancy and more aggressive management of pregnancy and birth. A few examples can usefully be given to highlight the consequences of this. It is generally the case that women who are pregnant will behave during their pregnancy in ways designed to maximise the welfare of the developing foetus. Women may, for example, stop smoking, reduce their alcohol intake, avoid dangerous pursuits or eschew pharmaceutical products. However, some women may not - either as a deliberate choice or because of social or other pressures. It was ever thus. However, the capacity to visualise the foetus in the womb, and the notion that the foetus is now a patient, have increasingly resulted in interventions in women's lifestyle choices in the course of pregnancy. The pressure, therefore, is on the pregnant woman to put the foetus before herself, even though the foetus has no legal personality or standing and the woman does. Certainly, we may hope that women would do this, especially if it involves minimal intrusion into their own lives, but we should be careful to distinguish here between what we regard as morally acceptable behaviour on the woman's part, and what we would wish legally to enforce.

Recent years have seen an increase in the legal imposition on women of foetus-friendly behaviour, even though the woman could not be forced into similar behaviour if the foetus was in fact a born child with the full panoply of legal rights. Thus, women have been incarcerated during pregnancy because their behaviour was thought likely to harm the foetus, but had the child been born they would have no obligation to use their own bodies to save that child's life, say by donating a kidney, or blood or bone marrow. And women's choices are also sometimes ignored. Perhaps the most poignant example of this is the American case of Angela Carder.[43]

Mrs Carder had suffered from leukaemia, which was in remission when she married and became pregnant. Tragically in the course of the pregnancy the leukaemia returned aggressively and it was clear that she was terminally ill. At about 26 weeks into the pregnancy, her doctors decided that it would be possible to salvage the foetus were Mrs Carder to undergo a Caesarean section. This Mrs Carder refused. Although legally irrelevant, she had the support both of her husband and her family in making that decision. In spite of her objections, the doctors sought and obtained the authority of a court to proceed with the surgery. Neither Mrs Carder nor the child survived. Although this decision was subsequently overturned on appeal,[44] by then the cruel act had been carried out.

Equally, there has been a trend (which thankfully may now have been stopped[45]) of aggressive intervention in decisions at the moment of birth. In the case of *Re S*,[46] for example, a woman was forced to deliver by Caesarean section after doctors decided that both she and her foetus were at risk of dying unless this was carried out. The woman protested that she had religious objections to the surgery, but a judge (after a hearing of approximately 20 minutes) authorised the surgery to go ahead. What is of additional interest in these cases is that the interests of the foetus are given some standing even though technically it has no rights, and technically the woman is free to make her own choices about her own bodily integrity. In no other circumstance would a competent individual be forced to undergo unwanted surgery.[47]

As Lord Browne-Wilkinson said in the case of *Airedale NHS Trust* v *Bland*:[48]

'Any treatment given by a doctor to a patient which is invasive (ie involves any interference with the physical integrity of the patient) is unlawful unless done with the consent of the patient; it constitutes the crime of battery and the tort of trespass to the person.'[49]

Conclusion

This necessarily brief analysis of some aspects of pregnancy and birth would seem to suggest that what might in the past have been essentially uncomplicated in legal and ethical respects has become increasingly complex. Indeed, there is now as much attention focussed on what happens before birth as there is on birth itself, but it is necessary to consider these matters as part of the phenomenon of birth, as they will all impact on whether, how and in what condition we are actually born.

This is not necessarily a bad thing, but it has raised important legal and ethical questions. In the contemporary world pregnancies are created in novel ways, and children are born into novel family units. Pregnancies can be interrupted for clinical or social reasons. We can no longer take it for granted that the woman who gives birth to a child is its biological mother - a change which rocks the fundamental assumptions of centuries.

All in all, what in the past might have appeared to be an easy (legally and ethically if not physically) moment in life's journey has become a legal and ethical minefield, both for children in some cases, and for women in many cases. The apparent expansion of choices in conception and pregnancy has arguably complicated the natural event of birth. Momentous changes have occurred over the last 25 years or so, which challenge both the assumption that the birth of a child is always a blessing and the very nature of the nuclear family itself - a unit which the United Nations regards as the fundamental cornerstone of society. From being an essentially private matter, birth has increasingly been rendered part of the public sphere, with the consequence that state intervention becomes more likely and more frequent. This is a paradoxical conclusion given the western world's strong desire to distance itself from the eugenic policies of the last century. Oddly, advances in medicine may have inadvertently resulted in the re-politicisation of birth - arguably an unfortunate conclusion in respect of what has been jealously guarded as a private affair. Legal recognition of human rights has also contributed to creating tensions about status and compensation. As they say, there is no action without a reaction - food for thought when considering this area.

[1] see Glover J 'Causing Death and Saving Lives', Harmondsworth, Penguin, 1984

[2] [1981] 1 All ER 26

[3] Congenital Disabilities (Civil Liability) Act 1976

[4] Scottish Law Commission, 'Liability for Antenatal Injury', Cmnd 537/1973

[5] 'Injuries to Unborn Children', Law Commission Report no 60, Cmnd 5709/1974; for further discussion, see Pace, P.J., 'Civil Liability for Pre-Natal Injuries', 40 MLR 141 (1977)

[6] see note 3, *supra*

[7] Cmnd 7054

[8] see chapter 26

[9] see Teff, H. and Munro, C., 'Thalidomide: The Legal Aftermath', Farnborough, Saxon House, 1976

[10] see, for example, cases such as *Emeh* v *Kensington and Chelsea and Westminster AHA* [1984] 3 All ER 1044 (CA) and *Thake* v *Maurice* [1986] 1 All ER 497 (CA)

[11] this term is used here as a catch-all to include wrongful conception and wrongful pregnancy. An explanation of why this might not be uncontroversial can be found in Mason J K and McCall Smith, RA, 'Law and Medical Ethics', (5th Ed), London, Butterworths, 1999, but it will suffice for these purposes. See also, Dickens, B., 'Wrongful Birth and Life, Death Before Birth', in McLean, S.A.M.,(ed) 'Legal Issues in Human Reproduction', Aldershot, Gower, 1989

[12] precluded apparently by the terms of the Congenital Disabilities (Civil Liability) Act 1976 s 1(2)(b); see Law Commission report, note 4, *supra*, paragraph 89. The common law position in England and Wales is illustrated by the case of *McKay* v *Essex AHA* [1982] 2 All ER 771 (CA)

[13] 1998 SC 389

[14] (2000) 52 B.M.L.R. 1

[15] see Dickens, note 11 *supra*

[16] but see Fortin J 'Is the "Wrongful Life" Action Really Dead?' [1987] JSWL 306

[17] Article 2.1

[18] for further discussion, see Lee R G and Morgan D 'Human Fertilisation and Embryology; Regulating the Reproductive Revolution', London, Blackstone Press, 2001, particularly at p. 44

[19] Edwards R and Sharpe D 'Social Values and Research in Human Embryology' (1971) 231 *Nature* 87 at p.87

[20] for discussion, see McLean S A M 'The Right to Reproduce', in Campbell et al (eds, 'Human Rights: From Rhetoric to Reality', Oxford, Basil Blackwell, 1986

[21] for further discussion, see Meyers D 'The Human Body and the Law', Edinburgh UP, 1970, chapter 2

[22] *Skinner* v *Oklahoma* 316 US 535 (1942)

[23] *Orford* v *Orford* (1921) 59 DLR 251

[24] Human Fertilisation and Embryology Act 1990 s 28

[25] s 31

[26] for example, Sweden

[27] [1997] 2 All ER 687

[28] see McLean S A M 'Consent and the Law: Review of the Current Provisions in the Human Fertilisation and Embryology Act 1990', DoH, September 1997 (Consultation Document); 'Review of the Common Law Provisions Relating to the Removal of Gametes and of the Consent Provisions in the Human Fertilisation and Embryology Act 1990', DoH, July 1998 (Final Report)

[29] see generally Schedule 3 to the Act

[30] for discussion see Consultation Document, note 24, *supra*

[31] Cmnd 9314/1984, paras 4.4 and 10.9

[32] 'Human Fertilisation and Embryology: A Framework for Legislation', Cm 259/1987. The Government, however, declined to make this unlawful (para 59) although it shared the Warnock Committee's view that it should not be encouraged

[33] 1979 Article 2.1 which precludes discrimination on the grounds, amongst others, of birth

[34] para 3.4

[35] Human Fertilisation and Embryology (Deceased Fathers) Bill 2001

[36] para 3.7

[37] para 3.9

[38] BMA, 'Human Genetics: Choice and Responsibility', Oxford University Press, 1998, at p. 130

[39] ibid, at p. 52

[40] see, for example, the Masterton family who tragically lost their only daughter and have mounted a campaign to be permitted access to IVF and sex selection

[41] recently, the Hashmi family have also sought access to preimplantation genetic diagnosis to have a child of the correct sex to save the life of an existing, terminally ill child. See *The Times* 2 October 2001

[42] for further discussion, see Mattingley S S 'The maternal-fetal dyad: exploring the two-patient obstetric model', 'Hastings Center Report', 22, 13 (1992); Johnsen D 'The creation of fetal rights: conflicts with women's constitutional rights to liberty, privacy and equal protection', Yale Law J, 95, 599; McLean S A M 'Moral Status (Who or What Counts)?', in Bewley S and Ward R H (eds), 'Ethics in Obstetrics and Gynaecology', London, RCOG Press, 1994, 26

[43] Re AC 533 A 2d 611 (DC, 1987)

[44] 573 A 2d 1235 (1990)

[45] *Re MB (an adult: medical treatment)* [1997] 8 Med LR217

[46] *Re S* [1992] 4 All ER 671

[47] one way round this problem of course has been to declare that the woman in question was not in fact competent, either because of pre-existing personal circumstances (see Re MB [1997] 8 Med L R 217 – a woman was initially held to be lacking capacity because of a needle phobia) or because of the pain of labour and childbirth

[48] [1993] AC 789

[49] at p. 882

Childhood

Mary Riddell

Monday morning. Behind locked doors, the week begins at Oliver Goldsmith Primary School in Peckham. A Spanish pupil, aged around ten, is fetched from his classroom to interpret for a visiting father who speaks no English. A few yards away, in a reception hall monitored by closed-circuit television, a new boy with hair plaited in cornrows sits silently. The woman with him, not his mother, does not have his passport or birth certificate, and nobody seems to know which school he last attended. 'We want you here,' someone tells him. 'We just need to find some more details before you can start.' In the playground, a group of girls stares up at an autumn sky criss-crossed by vapour trails.

'We're plane-spotting,' they say. It is November 2001, and they have been counting jets since September 11. It seems to them that there are more than usual today. The teachers constantly offer reassurance that the school is not a target for terrorists, but it is easy to imagine that the children cannot think themselves inviolable. One year previously, Damilola Taylor left this playground for his after-school computer class. He died of stab wounds in a dank stairwell before he reached home.

Although the tragedy will not be forgotten, memories of Damilola were always destined to be ephemeral here. Among a roll of 611, there is 23 per cent mobility. 150 children started during this school year[1], and many will not stay long. Some pupils arrive from Africa or the Caribbean to live in London's promised land with uncles or aunts. Some stay briefly before disappearing back to their own country. Sometimes the school is never told that such ghost-children have gone.

Oliver Goldsmith pupils come from 40 different countries and speak almost as many languages. 45 per cent have special needs[2]. Only one child in the top class has been here since reception. The majority are poor. There is ample testimony in this playground to satisfy any outside observer with questions about what a British childhood means. Few ask. Before a recent revival, Oliver Goldsmith was the biggest and worst primary in Britain. Later it was Damilola's school. It remains a template of children's lives in the inner cities at the start of a new century. But this is not the parable of childhood that society wants to hear.

Who are Britain's children? What is modern childhood, and what are children for? They have never been so important: to a Government that puts their education, health and welfare at the heart of policy; to a society that frets over malign influences spanning paedophiles to big-brand advertisers; to parents who worry about everything from drugs to work-life imbalance. While having children gets less alluring, (by 2025, the UK population will have reached zero growth[3]) grown-up society has never seemed so enmeshed in children's lives. Equally, it has rarely appeared so estranged. Legally, culturally, socially and politically, children are segregated from adulthood. Their needs, their hopes and rights are filtered through the prism of an adult world. Neither politicians nor parents want to unravel the dreams of childhood from their own. Why would they? Children offer evidence of our failings but also some glimpse of our perfectibility. They are our second chance.

Investing children with romantic visions is nothing new. The work of Philippe Ariès, the French sociologist who suggested that childhood did not exist as a distinct cultural state until the 17th century,[4] is increasingly challenged now. The historian, Nicholas Orme, argues instead that medieval people, especially after the 12th century, had clear ideas of what childhood was, when it began and ended and how to make it joyous.[5] Nor does he accept the Ariès view that a high mortality rate made children's lives as expendable as they were to Montaigne, who observed that he had 'lost two or three children in their infancy, not without regret but without great sorrow.'[6] Whatever the merits of Ariès' thesis, he was the first to stake out childhood as a separate state. Children, he says, 'form the most conservative of human societies.'[7] The example he cites - plastic windmills on sticks, popular long after working mills disappeared from the countryside – may be arcane. It is also a reminder that for modern children, living in a kaleidoscope world shaken up by commercial pressures or poverty, by family upheaval and government initiatives, conservatism is a rationed luxury.

The separateness of children was refined by the 17th and 18th century philosophers whose ideas underpin current theories of child development. John Locke argued that the newborn is a *tabula rasa*, not sinful, as Christianity claimed, nor imbued with innate knowledge or morality, as Plato had it. Jean-Jacques Rousseau saw children as 'noble savages' born with a natural sense of right and wrong. The debate of nurture (Locke) versus nature (Rousseau) applies still to 21st century childhood. That label, however, bestows a false modernity. Through cultural inertia, or nostalgia, or fear, society's idea of childhood remains embedded in the past.

The notion that there was ever a golden age of childhood is patently wrong. Vague ideas of the Victorian era as a high watermark of innocence contrast oddly with Dickensian childcare, run under the auspices of Fagin and Mr Murdstone. Whether 'little mothers' or 'street arabs', Victorian children were expected to work. Despite some protective labour laws (in 1874, the legal age for a job in a textile factory was increased to ten and, in 1901, to 12),[8] the emphasis was on the child as aide or earner. Although the 1876 Elementary Education Act defined a child as under fourteen, some rural pupils left school before their eleventh birthday. The age of consent, applicable to girls only, was raised from 12 to 13 in 1875.[9] Literary Victorians had a shrewd idea of how (more privileged) youngsters think and of how adults fail to connect with that process. George Eliot's insights on the Tulliver children are enduringly acute:

'… so it comes that we can look on at the troubles of our children with a smiling disbelief in the reality of their pain. Is there anyone who can recover the experience of his childhood ..when it was so long from one Midsummer to another? What he felt when his schoolfellows shut him out of their game because he would pitch the ball wrong out of mere willfulness; or on a rainy day in the holidays when he didn't know how to amuse himself and fell from idleness into mischief, from mischief into defiance, and from defiance into sulkiness; or when his mother absolutely refused to let him have a tailed coat that 'half', although every other boy of his age had gone into tails already?'[10]

So much for the idea that Harry Enfield surliness or an obsession with branding are anything new. For tailed coats, read Nike trainers. But the lessons society takes from Victorian examples owe less to universals than to Little Nell mawkishness largely unconnected to the modern child. Today's small girls wear disco Lycra and glitter nail varnish. Pre-teen boys covet the right jacket from French Connection (seductively packaged in tissue paper and sealed with a sticker reading "Guaranteed FCUK"). Children eat McDonald's and, if rich enough, travel across Europe and beyond. Just as for Alice, drinking cordial or nibbling on a currant cake, their worlds grow small and large alternately. Children can still be beguiled by Lewis Carroll and by the almost equally old-fashioned magic of Harry Potter, but they are Microsoft converts too.

Children, conservative but unsentimental, move on. Grown-ups, suspicious of new, commercialised playthings are less adaptable. They, mourning lost tradition, on behalf of their children and themselves, hesitate to walk back through Carroll's looking glass. In an age when children supposedly grow old more quickly, adults are reluctant to grow old at all.

This chapter sets no precise age boundaries on childhood. (Nor does a legal system which decrees that a child can be found guilty of murder at the age of 10 but cannot buy a pet gerbil until she or he is 12.) Childhood begins in infancy and drifts towards some finishing post scarcely better-defined than in Victorian times. Many more students in higher education, and teenagers staying on with their parents - sometimes for home comforts, often because they can't afford to move out – makes some children dependent for longer. The popular emphasis, however, is on the brevity of childhood.

Nick Cohen, writing in The Observer,[11] cites Saatchi and Saatchi's estimate that the age cut-off point for buying toys falls by one year in every five: most children stop playing with Lego by the age of seven. Ogilvy and Mather report that the premature ageing of children is more striking in Britain than in any other developed country. While advertisers may exaggerate lucrative precocity, it is indisputable that adults seek to stave off getting old. Every miracle face cream, Botox jab, exercise programme and new motorbike offers them a stake in elastic, if not quite eternal, youth. Marketers devise new categories - kidults and middlescents - to describe the Formalin generation. There is nothing necessarily wrong in the banishment of such social stereotypes as the whiskery-chinned Giles grandma. A cult of youthfulness means that, in helpful ways, parents are less distanced from their children. The danger is that a generation which observes fluid rules about its own evolution is curiously inflexible about the changing patterns of children's lives.

Celebrating new skills, such as IT competence, often seems secondary to wishing children to be part of some halcyon age that never was. Nostalgia, in turn, feeds false ideas of innocence and evil. As Marina Warner said, in her Reith lectures: 'Children are perceived as innocent because they're outside society, pre-historical, pre-social, instinctual creatures of reason, primitive, kin to unspoiled nature. Whether this is seen as good or evil often reflects the self-image of the society.'[12]

When unsureness prevails and faith ebbs away from old institutions – religion, a largely discredited royal family, the state – children are made to fill the vacuum of certainty. They are symbols of goodness and virtue to adults who struggle to find such values in their own environment. As Warner recognized, the deviant behaviour of children can lead to [adult] 'disillusion, often punitive and callous .. because they [the young] betrayed an abstract myth about children's proper childlikeness.'[13] The case usually quoted to illustrate such a polarity is that of Robert Thompson and Jon Venables, who abducted and murdered James Bulger.

At nine, the children would have been too young even to know that death is the irreversible end to life. At ten, the age of both boys when they killed James, they were deemed old enough to face trial for murder in an adult court and receive an (almost) adult tariff of 15 years, applied by the then Home Secretary, Michael Howard, and subsequently ruled unlawful. When the trial ended, an adult mob yelled: 'Kill them; hang them' as if justice decreed that the blue police vans bearing them from court should be bound for Tyburn rather than council rehabilitation units.

If punishing 'evil' children reveals an ugly face of adulthood, then the homage paid to those acclaimed as pure is suspect too. Dead children are invariably beautiful. Sweet school pictures of girls like Lauren Wright, beaten to death by her stepmother, or Victoria Climbié, murdered by her great-aunt and the subject of a public inquiry, always provoke breast-beating from citizens and agencies, including those who failed them in their lifetimes. Serene images mask the reality of squalid, brutalised lives. Society likes its victims sanitised, scrubbed, angelic; and those who do not comply may get short shrift. A member of the child protection team in Haringey, north London, told the Climbié inquiry that she had not visited Victoria's home to check a nurse's suspicion of abuse because she was frightened of catching the skin disease, scabies. More broadly, it took until May 2000 for the Home Office to issue guidance that child prostitutes were victims of abuse, not criminals.

The dichotomy between good and evil impacts also on the 'normal' child. Not since Salem, Massachusetts, in the spring of 1692[14], has society seemed so fearful of malign influences on children. The death of Sarah Payne, an eight year old schoolgirl abducted and murdered during a holiday with her siblings and grandparents, provoked a name-and-shame campaign against paedophiles in the News of the World. In the subsequent witch-hunt, innocent men were hounded and a paediatrician had her house vandalised. Anger created by all manner of social ills on rundown housing estates seemed to find vent in this hysteria, legitimated by the vulnerability of children to hostile strangers. But most abuse takes place in the home. An NSPCC survey[15], billed as the most comprehensive undertaken in the UK, claimed that one in 14 young people are abused by a parent or carer and one in 100 had been sexually abused. In 2001, 65 children under seven were killed, mostly by their parents; an unexplained, 50% rise on the previous year. Killing and abuse by strangers is rare, but that does not prevent adults deeming children disproportionately at risk - not only from paedophiles but from other supposed agents of corruption.

Watching television will make children fat and sap their imagination. Junk food is guaranteed to harm them and make them unwitting disciples of globalisation. Shoot-'em-up computer games will predispose them to violence. Teen magazines will lure them into precocious sex, and clothing retailers will garb them for it. Some time ago, a marketing magazine[16] announced yet another new category of person. 'Tweenagers' is the adspeak invented for eight to twelve year olds with large amounts of disposable income and the power to influence their families' choice of products, from breakfast cereal to cars. Eight to 16 year olds in the UK are thought to spend £50 million a year on music alone. A recent report claimed that 'housewives' buy six out of ten products on the edict of their 'tweenage' children.[17]

Obviously, advertisers love to play up the impact of rapacious mini-consumers with 'pester power'. It's a gospel that boosts sales. More interesting is adults' easy acceptance that children are so susceptible to influences ranging from screen violence to aggressive marketers. On the first point, researchers have found it hard to prove any causal link between moderately violent television and damagingly aggressive behaviour. Nor is there much precedent for thinking children are at overwhelming risk of being harmed or tainted.

Gory imagery has been constructed, down the centuries, expressly for children. From the brothers Grimm, through the black, cautionary tales of Belloc and Hoffman, to Philip Pullman, the first children's author to win the Whitbread Prize, child fiction has been dovetailed to the supposed primitivism of its audience. Now, bizarrely, large elements of a society that has always deemed children robust enough to absorb gruesome influences, suddenly thinks the young are stripped of cultural immunity.

The reason that children are seen as so vulnerable and corruptible connects with adults' own terrors. In his book, Paranoid Parenting, Frank Furedi claims to identify a generation of neurotics, frightened by childcare gurus and politicians into delusions of inadequacy, guilt and failure. It is true that most parental worries are deracinated from actual risk. Unicef research[18] shows that British children are, apart from their Swedish counterparts, the least likely in the developed world to die from deliberate or unintentional injury. Even the widespread assumption that children suffer from parents' long hours looks over-hyped. According to a survey in Top Sante magazine[19], three-quarters of working mothers believe that children suffer when both parents work full-time. Yet Furedi[20] quotes International Labour Organisation indicators that the average full-time working day in Britain increased by only 1.7 minutes between 1980 and 1997.

Of course, many more women work now. A long-hours culture is to be deplored, and flexible working for parents is desirable. Even so, it would not be too cynical to think the worries of Top Sante readers may be fuelled more by their own oppressive schedules than by any knock-on effects to their children. Adult angst gets displaced on to the young, who, if asked, say that they too would like more time. Adults invariably suppose this means they want more of their parents' attention, and in many cases this will be so. But perhaps some children would also like less close focus; fewer swimming, music, judo or ballet classes; more space to live in an imagined world that ambitious parents wish for and violate in equal part.

In America, the crucible of child-focussed neurosis, parents can spy on their babies through a daycare webcam before parking them in front of a 'Baby Einstein' video, exposing infants to classical music, poetry and foreign languages. With sales running at more than a million a year, a similar version, 'Baby Bright', arrived in Britain in November 2001, claiming, with expert endorsement, that it would 'develop the cognitive processes of the brain' in children of three months and over.

As counterweight to the evidence of over-anxious, pushy parents, Furedi attempts to explode the supposed myth of the 'at risk' child. It is correct, as he says, that children have 'a formidable capacity for resilience'[21] It is also true (as he does not say) that society, in fretting over children who are not at risk, conveniently ignores those who are. Adults worry about the wrong children. The most resilient are, absurdly, deemed the most vulnerable. Extreme agonising over schooling, development and safety is largely, though not exclusively, the pastime of the pampered classes. Does exposure to screen violence damage a secure child whose parents do not beat each other up? Unlikely.

Advertising may be banal, irritating and opportunistic, but how much does it harm or even corrupt young children? At a meeting to float ideas for this chapter, brands and consumerism were, overwhelmingly, the issues that most disturbed the (adult) audience. Yet every parent also knows that the age of conformism is brief. By his or her early teens, a child once in thrall to the 'right' labels may choose a more idiosyncratic (and cheaper) style. Shopping at Oxfam is often the luxury of the well-off child, whose unwillingness to be defined by possessions is bolstered by boredom with the easily-available. The real brand victims are poorer children incited by marketers to crave the unaffordable. One researcher studying branding reported a little boy trying to write Reebok in Biro on an old chainstore trainer.

That small example indicates a wider gulf. In post-millennial Britain, it is misleading to talk of childhood in the singular. There are two different childhoods going on. In the poor child's model, millions are at risk. They will have more physical and mental illness, do worse at school, run a greater danger of being jobless, commit and suffer more crime. They will die earlier. Somehow, their needs have been eclipsed in Pony Clubbish clamour over how children's lives should be moulded by adults. Parental determinism may be a myth. Social determinism is not.

When the Blair government came to power, child poverty was the worst in the EU. One in three children was poor. In 2001, that statistic still applied, despite the government's specific pledge: to reduce child poverty by a quarter by 2004, to halve it by 2010 and to eradicate it by 2020. As the Chancellor, Gordon Brown, said: 'We must never forget that poverty – above all the poverty of children – disfigures not just the lives of the poor but all our society.' Yet even before the Labour party conference of 2001, many in the voluntary sector were beginning to fear that that pressure to improve public services, principally health and education, would impel Blair to move child poverty down the list of priorities. An economic downturn threatened. The war in Afghanistan began. Even the heavy hint, in November 2001, of a move to higher taxation offered no automatic guarantees to poor children.

The potential fault line between government rhetoric and achievement had been obvious from the outset. Social justice in Britain (unlike, say, in Sweden) is always seen as a camp-follower of economic buoyancy. Expensive solutions tend to be for good times only. Besides, Blair's ambitions looked more costly than the government had explained or even, perhaps, grasped. In a report for the IPPR[22], Peter Robinson claimed that meeting the goals would entail a revenue cost equal to 0.6 per cent of GDP by 2002, with the implication that 'eliminating child poverty completely may cost something up to another 1.5 per cent of

GDP.' Since current policies have lifted those closest to the poverty line, Robinson expected the cost to be higher. Separate research suggests that 1.5 million extra jobs would be needed to take one million children out of poverty through the work-based route favoured by government.[23]

In August 2001, the Child Poverty Action Group (CPAG) attacked government 'hypocrisy' on child poverty and deplored its refusal to overhaul the social fund, designed to help the very poorest. A few weeks earlier, the CPAG had cast doubt on the assertion that one million children had already been lifted out of poverty. On the government's own figures,[24] the drop, from 4.5 million in1998/99 to 4.3 million in 1999/2000, was a much more modest 200,000. Even allowing for the fact that more substantial results towards the end of the period would have come too late for inclusion, the results looked disappointing.

Measuring child poverty is, possibly fortuitously for policy-makers, hardly more precise than sculpting blancmange. The relative yardstick used - income below 50 per cent of the average - may illustrate a (widening) income gap rather than deepening absolute poverty. There is, however, no doubt that millions of British children are deprived and excluded. Unicef's league tables of relative and of absolute poverty in the developed world[25] places Britain fourth from bottom in the first category (Italy, the US and Mexico were lower), and sixth from lowest in the second, beating only Italy, Spain, the Czech Republic, Hungary and Poland.

Labour does deserve credit for acknowledging the scandal of child poverty and introducing some remedies. In December 2001, a report claimed that exclusion indicators were encouraging, although poverty levels remained stubbornly high.[26] Changes to tax and benefits and schemes such as SureStart have been helpful, but social justice, undeliverable on the cheap, will require major redistribution and income tax rises. On measures already promised, the integrated child credit (not fixed at the time of writing) needs to be high enough to make a significant impact on poverty.

There are other issues. Childcare, one of the less successful crusades of the Blair government, has offered - in the place of vaunted affordability and excellence - a ramshackle model supplying, in 2001, registered places for only one in seven children under eight in England. It is unclear how, when provision is so patchy, and when a typical private nursery place in London costs £135 a week,[27] poorer mothers are supposed to do as the Chancellor hopes and get a job.

As the Daycare Trust argues, there is a compelling argument for a Childcare Agency and for a countrywide web of children's centres offering services for all ages. For an estimated £1bn capital spending over 10 years and an annual budget of £2.5 bn,[28] British children - irrespective of class or wealth or creed - could have what is accorded to their European counterparts as a birthright: a fair system and a more equal chance.

Meanwhile the rhetoric of 'the many, not the few' has possibly lulled the conscience-ridden of Middle England into the view that the difference between rich and poor childhoods is not as great as all that. The mantra of universally high standards, in schools particularly, carries the subliminal message that differences are nuanced. The most cursory look at a top-ranking primary in, say, Islington or Clapham and an equivalent school in a poor area, such as Peckham, shows how wide those disparities are.

Some time has passed since Oliver Goldsmith School was described by an Ofsted inspector as 'being like something out of Dante's inferno.' Over four years, and under a new head, Mark Parsons, it has lost its 'most notorious' tag. Its SATS results for 11 year-olds, once catastrophic, have doubled in percentage terms for both of the last two years, and classroom fights and Pokemon protection rackets are non-existent now. But the narrative has inevitably been driven by the terrible death of Damilola Taylor. Parsons was so disturbed by subsequent, incorrect reports about bullying at his school that he retreated from media contact. His interview for this chapter was the only one he gave as the first anniversary of Damilola's killing approached.

There are, as Parsons says, no teachers' or doctors' children here. Most of his pupils just miss the cut of free school dinners, 'a very bad measure of poverty' and the determinant of whether a head gets extra funding of around £400 a year per pupil. A large number of Parsons' most challenging children don't qualify. Many speak no English when they start, and some have been shipped around the world - social freight bound for a spoiled Utopia. 'Children come over here and can't go out. There are issues on child-on-child crime. They're restricted and uncared for by the community. Their parents are in shock. This school doesn't fail children. Society does. I've taught in schools where teachers say they aren't a social service. They don't say that here. We have to be.

'Children like these should not be educated in a school of 600 pupils. I wouldn't have any child in a school with more than a two-form entry [or around 480 pupils]…The British treat their children badly. Always have. We don't seem to love children, and I don't know why. Most schools like this have an overwhelming duty of care, and we don't fund them well enough. Ideally, you need no more than 20 children in a junior class and 16 in an infant one. With those numbers, I could really produce the goods. We do phenomenally well, but it's difficult to work with 30 children with so many difficulties and so many different languages. I've got classes with 22 special needs kids and four with English as a special language.'[29] The polarity between rich and poor children is, in his view, getting worse.

A portrait of Damilola Taylor in his school sweatshirt hangs in Parsons' office. Outside, in the yard, the children wear identical uniform. They flutter round Parsons, ask if they are going to be in the football team and call him 'Sir.' This is a formal school with an emphasis on good behaviour and a disciplinarian culture. Parsons deals with fighting by offering one warning, followed by a short exclusion. It is not a policy designed to appeal to liberals. He says it has helped eradicate 'chaos.'

By lunchtime a huddle of miscreants is gathered outside his office. In the playground, the odd child weeps and clings to him. Some of the pupils here are needy, he says. Some are hungry. Even on a SATS test day, barely half have had breakfast, but most look bright and hopeful. Children almost always do. There is hardly a single white face in a wave of youngsters crammed into too small a yard. Last time Ofsted called, they asked where the playing field was.

Education, education, education. Oliver Goldsmith School, and hundreds more in the inner cities, are the unmarked junctions at which political rhetoric and reality collide. When circumstances seem so bleak to Parsons, a successful head, it is hard to be optimistic for less good schools; the incubator, though not the cause, of difficult lives. Britain's facility for turning out the wrong sort of children is a source of national bafflement. How come that we have the highest teenage pregnancy rate in Europe, with 2,200 babies born a year to girls of 14 or under?[30] Why is a wave of robbery, burglary and theft committed by school-age children during school hours? Why are 50,000 children playing truant on any given day, according to DfES estimates?[31]

One answer lies in social divisions. New research[32] shows that, while British teenagers are among the most able in the world, there is a closer link between high achievement and social background than in most other countries. However the blame gets parcelled out, the cures have a negative ring. Most initiatives - an exclusion order, a curfew, a detention, a parenting order, a (disgraceful but government-blessed) slap for an infant - are hammered out on the anvil of punishment or prevention. Policy is rarely designed to illuminate children's lives. A rigid curriculum promotes attainment, but undiluted targets and testing have a pinched feel. When the aim is to secure the minimum possible failure rate with the minimum possible investment, the likely result is obvious. We are creating the minimum child.

At best, the minimum child does fine. At worst, she or he will follow a slow lane route to teenage pregnancy or one of the cruel and unusual young offender institutions that so appal the Lord Chief Justice, Lord Woolf, and the former Chief Inspector of Prisons, Sir David Ramsbotham. Being poor may not automatically pre-ordain bad outcomes. But no government can ever create good education and health services without first alleviating poverty.

This government opted, particularly in its first term, to shuffle as much blame as feasible on to 'bad' parents. Research linking juvenile offending with lack of supervision heralded[33] unprecedented state control. When parenting gets politicised, children - like the Tube or a decaying hospital - become fodder for Public Private Partnerships. Long after the Blair government stepped back from openly promoting marriage, there was a sense that some ministers brooded, as dolefully as Miss Havisham in her dusty bridal lace, on how things might have been.

If the state is too eager to meddle in children's lives, parents are often too diffident. In an age of fracturing relationships, only five per cent of children are given a full explanation of their parents' separation and encouraged to ask questions, according to a survey for the Joseph Rowntree Foundation[34]. Although children of ten drew a clear distinction between biological and step-family members, they were also adaptable. Over half regarded living in two households with some positive feelings, such as loving a new baby brother or sister but being pleased to escape for a peaceful weekend. Being hopeful and happy was directly linked to being given some choice in how much time they spent in different homes. In a separate study, the foundation found that children preferred 'kinship care' - being looked after by extended family, normally grandparents - to fostering or residential homes. The authors urged government to offer its support.[35]

Of the 50 children interviewed, many said that they felt safe and loved and settled with their relatives, most of whom were over fifty. They were able to keep links with siblings and friends and sustain their racial and cultural heritage. These children's views were expressed at a time when foster parents are in short supply and the state's parenting record is in tatters. Among 58,000 children in the charge of local authorities, 70 per cent of those fostered or in care homes leave school at 16 with no qualifications. Only four per cent get five or more GCSEs at grade C or above, compared with a national average of nearly 50 per cent.

Children who have been in care are more than twice as likely to become teenage parents and at greater risk of being unemployed and homeless. More than a quarter of prisoners were in care as children, as against two per cent of the general population. The Blair government, slightly vaguely, has promised action. As the authors of the kinship report[36] suggest, ministers would do well to listen, in this arena as in many others, to what children want.

Theirs is mostly the forgotten voice when families collapse and alter. Although the divorce rate peaked in 1993, two in five marriages will end. Many more people are cohabiting. 1.7 million British families, or almost a quarter, are headed by a lone parent.[37] Access for absent parents (of whom 97 per cent are fathers) often remains difficult. When unmarried couples break up, children have none of the financial rights the law accords to divorcees. Public muddle extends to the private sphere. Modern parents' explanations of their divorces to their children often seem as furtive and as sketchy as a Victorian matriarch's masterclass on sex.

Why do we misread children and under-estimate their good sense, their resilience and their moral competence? Why does society fret over them so constantly and understand them so little? As if constructing a house without a plan, we don't even know what the result is supposed to look like. In a report on European daycare, Peter Moss sketches the particular way different nationalities view their very young children. The French child is 'seen as a future adult citizen, who must be integrated into the larger community via the acquisition of French culture and republican values.'[38] The Swedish child, conversely, is the Dahlberg model of 'an active and creative actor, as a subject and citizen .. a child worth listening to and having a dialogue with, and who has the courage to think and act by himself…'[39]

What do Britons want? We're not sure. Negatively, we want our children not to be pregnant at 12, not to be bullied, not delinquent, not to be mugged for a mobile phone, not disappointed. On the positive side, we long for them to be happy, clever, successful. Both the plus and the minus columns of the wish-list are amorphous. They hint at how adults would like children to emerge relative to parental standards and to other citizens. They do not record what precise vision adult society has in mind, let alone serve children's dreams of their own futures.

In 1998 Professor Bernard Crick prevailed on the then education secretary, David Blunkett, to begin to fill that gap. An advisory group report[40] declared as its aim 'a change in the political culture of this country: for people to think of themselves as active citizens, willing, able and equipped to have an influence on public life.' Crick's aims - a broad grounding in the humanities and what he called 'political literacy', plus community involvement and public service - were enshrined in a course for 11 to 16 year olds. Despite a recognized need to inform children, and not just to cram them, civil servants were, at the time of writing, pressing the education secretary, Estelle Morris, to keep citizenship teaching as cursory as possible, despite evidence that a rigid curriculum may be counter-productive.

The Prince's Trust[41] found that young offenders and those at risk of turning to crime felt constantly judged and assessed at school and complained that teachers did not understand their needs. The emphasis on the child as performer can produce, by obvious corollary, the child as reject or excludee. At primary school, boys are almost ten times more likely to be excluded than girls.[42] Black children are excluded from school six times more often than white ones, and African Caribbean boys run the highest risk of all. They are eight times as likely to be banned, temporarily or permanently, as their white counterparts. In these circumstances it is all too easy for discrimination to become entrenched.

The law affecting children is particularly skewed. The age of criminal responsibility in England and Wales is ten; much lower than in most European countries. A child can be strip-searched at that age, although she may not be interviewed by the police until she is 12. She can fly a plane at 16 (but not drive a car until 17), drink alcohol at five (but not buy a hamster for another seven years). Such discrepancies reflect more than the tangled knitting of the law. They suggest that children are accorded smaller worth. Ten years after the landmark Children Act was brought into force, in October 1991, there has been no further great step forward in balancing out the rights of parent, child and state.

For every good decision, such as Lord Scarman's ruling that, in medical treatment, a parent must yield to a competent child,[43] there is some new assault on basic rights. The government decision, in November 2001, not to follow Scotland's lead towards making it illegal to smack small children, provoked widespread outrage that it should be lawful to hit a baby but not an adult. The decision, in the same month, to compile a police database of children as young as three who, officers feared, might one day become criminals, dismayed civil liberties groups.

No wonder children think themselves sidelined. Research by the children's rights organisation, Article 12 (from the UN Convention on the Rights of the Child), found only one in three children felt listened to by her family. A quarter said they had no say in schools, two thirds had no involvement in the community, and young disabled people complained that they had little discretion on anything, from choice of friends to the clothes they wanted to wear.

In January 2002, ministers announced a new army of special advisers: children of eleven upwards, recruited to offer "firm and frank advice" on how young Britain is being let down on crime, schools, runaways and other issues. It was the first significant response to increasing calls for children's rights to be enshrined in the political agenda. Before the last election, Barnardo's, the NSPCC and the Child Poverty Action Group issued a (so far little-heeded) five-point demand, including independent children's commissioners, a Cabinet minister for children and a greater voice for children on issues affecting them. If the government is beginning to realise that there are no greater experts on childhood than children themselves, that shift suggests some hope of progress.

But other forces are bearing down on childhood. Its boundaries are constantly redrawn, and its domain dwindles as British children become a shrinking species. Increasing numbers of adults don't want children at all. The birthrate of 2.40 in the 1970s is down a third to 1.66. In 1940, one in ten women did not have children; now that figure is up to one in four. In a Prospect essay,[44] Laurie and Matthew Taylor harked back to Joseph Schumpeter's view of half a century ago that adults were becoming aware of the heavy sacrifices parenthood involved and deciding not to bother. The Taylors also argued that the capacity to pass on name, position, occupation, even moral code, has been 'subverted in the modern world.' To make child-bearing attractive again, we must realise that, 'post-God and post-socialism', we need something to connect us to each other, to the future and to the public realm.

In order to acquire more of this social glue, the Taylors recommended encouraging people to have children by forging a more family-friendly society. Although this is an admirable aim, there may be a limited connection between a shortage of highchairs in the Savoy Grill and a plummeting birthrate. True, the British are peculiarly hostile to children. But Sweden is among the most family-friendly places on earth, and the birthrate there, at 1.5, is dropping even more steeply than here. Perhaps the electively barren are mostly, as the Taylors think, in thrall to 'individual self-fulfilment.' But that supposes that people once bore children out of altruism, when - from Bethlehem onwards - having babies has been inextricably linked with parental interests.

In modern Britain, we don't need children as slaves or soldiers or nannies or servants or inheritors of the family business - let alone as architects of a Judaeo-Christian world. However niggardly the state, adults don't need to breed people to keep them in their old age, to bury them when they die or vicariously to fulfil their dreams. There is nothing alluring in the old notion of the bred-for-purpose child. But new and whimsical reasons for parenthood seem no less cynical. Although a small minority of women might choose a child as a lifestyle accessory or a prop for a failing marriage, better reasons are also in short supply. Children have become an optional extra. Ironically, society needs them more than ever, to support a growing population of the old. The fact that this imperative has almost no impact on individual thinking demonstrates the blinkered attitude of a presentist age and illustrates how feeble notions of community have become.

A baby has always been the fulfilment of individuals' longing. The complementary idea of an infant as a separate entity quickly assimilated into a life beyond his or her parents' sole control is fading. When playing in the street is deemed dangerous, it is harder for a child to be independent. When there is no nearby grandma to run errands for, it is harder to be useful. When paid work is frowned upon or outlawed, it is harder to be self-reliant. In making children more protected, we have rendered them less free.

We have also reclassified them. Adults feel under no obligation now to have children, for their own fulfilment or for the greater good. Defining babies as a luxury rather than a necessity should make them more desirable. Why are they less so?

Part of the answer lies in the myth of altruism. Still, adults think of sleepless nights and ravaged bank balances and deem themselves virtuous to consider having children. This assumption of selflessness sits oddly with battalions of middle class parents struggling to get their offspring into the best schools, at the expense of everyone else's children. The problem, however, is not that we lack unselfish instincts. It is that we have ditched our selfish ones. The impulse to have babies, once necessity vanished, was the simple fact that children enhance the lives of their parents and others and bring them joy. When need has gone and delight gets discarded, then children truly do become redundant.

The idea spreads of the child as a burden. Children are portrayed in the media as expensive, career-stifling and almost certain to cause trouble, however they turn out. The aggressive child is a source of parental guilt, but so is the bullied victim. The precocious 10 year-old worries adults who, conversely, expect a tantrum-throwing three year-old to behave in a grown-up way. On the more useful side, children are exploited as a justification for whatever adults do. When the bombing of Afghanistan began, one national newspaper devoted its front page to a picture of two orphans of the Twin Towers atrocity. 'At war for children like these,' said a banner headline implying that only the monstrous would fail to fight in the name of such innocents.

Propaganda apart, our protective instincts are crude and uncertain. Many parents, understandably, refused the MMR jab because, despite years of clinical use and much research, they did not believe government assertions that it was safe. Neither informed scientific opinion that there was no linkage with autism or bowel disease, nor political pressure, nor the argument that private choice must sometimes be sublimated to the public good prevailed on doubters. Their resistance remained solid even after low-take up rates of the triple vaccine were followed by the outbreaks of measles doctors had predicted.

Risk is seen through a distorting glass. Children have more eating disorders, more mental health problems, more depression. More of them commit suicide. Yet adult worries are focussed elsewhere; on brands, on junk food, on commercialism. Undesirable as these may be, there are worse agents of harm. But pressures applied by family and state get ignored in favour of a shopping list of risk that is doubly calming for the adults who devise it. First, they are absolved from blame if damage to children can all be pinned on global Bluebeards, malign television programmers and other, insuperable outside forces. Second, claiming that children are spoiled and over-indulged is less disturbing than confronting deprivation. Happy children vastly outnumber the desperate. Even so, too many are poor. Too few can rely on a secure environment or on honesty in times of change. None has sufficient rights.

And, all the time, the notion disappears of childhood as a separate state, subject to its own rules. Of those, a principal standard is equality. No four year-old can tell a lie. All three year-olds offered one sweet now or a whole bag in ten minutes will opt for instant gratification. For children, the present is the only time that counts. 'Childhood has no forebodings,' George Eliot wrote.[45] 'But then; it is soothed by no memories of outlived sorrow.' Childhood, especially for the very young, is a world with no future and no past. It is starved of hope.

Grown-ups have always had to supply that deficit; to smooth the present while unveiling glimpses of how a safe and reassuring future might look. That makes it bizarre, dangerous even, for today's adults - out of love, protectiveness, nostalgia or guilt - to hark back to museum dreams of childhood. That vision conjures up a Singer Sargent portrait of light-bathed little girls with lamps and smocks. Carnation, Lily, Rose; gate-keepers of a simpler world. In the old fairytale, the chicken felt an acorn bounce off its head and shouted that the sky was collapsing. Children look different now, and so does folklore. In an inner city playground, in the second year of the century, little girls stare up at an autumn sky criss-crossed by aeroplane vapour trails and wait for the heavens to crash.

Children have changed. They have acquired the accessories of an era where knowledge exceeds comprehension across all generations. They are fearful, cynical, disillusioned, stressed and knowing. Or that is how hand-wringing traditionalists prefer to see them. Bring back innocence, right-wingers cry, certain that Railway Children values can be reinstated once the evils of sex and commerce are routed. Bring back authority, they say, almost as if cruel old regimes of tawse and terror tactics might be preferable to forging a new compact of discipline based on mutual respect. Wishing to rebottle discredited genies is a sign of adult confusion.

Grown-up opinion, as enshrined in the agencies of the state, wants children to inhabit a world of dreams and imagination, while following an iron school curriculum. It requires children to be responsible citizens but offers them few rights. It sets them at the heart of policy, yet accords them little voice. And, all the time, adults fail to see, in parodying children as sophisticated strangers, that knowingness has made them more vulnerable, not less so. That frailty is imposed not by an adult hit-list of avoidable risk but by a new culture of insecurity.

Even relatively sheltered British children are witness not only to the particular horrors of childhood, such as bullying, but also to all the demons of the adult world. In an information age, a parent's wish totally to cocoon a child from dangers spanning drugs on offer at the school gates to terrorism on the news, is neither achievable nor sensible. The old authoritarian toolkit of surveillance, prohibition and disapproval doesn't work. There is no option left but a better dialogue, in private and in public, with children. They are more responsible than adults ever understand.

They are also less altered. And, where they have evolved, those changes are, in the main, desirable, not threatening. In an age of temptation and uncertainty, it vital for children to become a trace less innocent; a fraction more wise. If adults can harness that wisdom, not suppress or fear it, then society can start to reclaim childhood.

Sally Waples assisted in the research for this paper.

---

[1] Author interview
[2] Author interview
[3] U.S. Census Bureau, 2000
[4] Ariès P 'Centuries Of Childhood', Jonathan Cape, 1962
[5] Orme N 'Medieval Children', Yale University Press, 2001
[6] Montaigne M 'Essais', II,8
[7] Ariès P, op cit, p. 68

[8] Davin A 'Growing Up Poor', Rivers Oram Press, 1996

[9] Davin A, op cit, p. 4

[10] Eliot G 'The Mill On The Floss' 1860, p122/3, Penguin English Library 1979

[11] Cohen N *The Observer*, Sept 2001

[12] Warner M 'Managing Monsters: Six Myths of Our Time', p35, 1994

[13] Warner M op cit, p. 44

[14] Miller A 'The Crucible'

[15] BMRM International for the NSPCC, Nov 2000

[16] Fry A *Mediaweek*, May 2001

[17] Mintel, 2001

[18] Innocenti Report Card, Issue 2, February 2001

[19] Top Sante, June 2001

[20] Furedi F 'Paranoid Parenting', p. 80, Allen Lane, 2001

[21] Furedi F, op cit, p. 25

[22] Robinson P 'Time To Choose Justice', Sept 2001, pp. 18&19

[23] Robinson, op cit, pp 18&19, quoting Piachaud and Sutherland, 2000

[24] Households Below Average Income (HBAI) statistics; Department of Work and Pensions, July 2001

[25] Innocenti Report Card, Issue No 1, June 2000

[26] Rahman, Palmer, Kenway 'Monitoring Poverty and Social Exclusion' New Policy Institute and Rowntree Foundation; December 2001

[27] 'All Our Futures', Daycare Trust, April 2001

[28] Holtermann S 'Children's Centres' Daycare Trust, June 2001

[29] Author interview

[30] 'Teenage pregnancy' (Summary), Social Exclusion Unit, 1999

[31] 'Preventing Social Exclusion', Social Exclusion Unit, March 2001

[32] 'Programme For International Student Assessment', OECD, December 2001

[33] 'Young People And Crime', Home Office Research Study 145, Graham and Bowling, 1995

[34] Dunn and Deater-Deckard 'Children's Views Of Their Changing Families', 2001

[35] Broad, Hayes, Rushforth 'Kith And Kin', December 2001

[36] Broad, Hayes, Rushforth, op cit

[37] 'One Parent Families Today - The Facts', National Council For One Parent Families; Sept 2001

[38] Moss P, op cit, p. 9

[39] Moss P, op cit (Dahlberg, 1997:22) p. 9

[40] 'Education For Citizenship And The Teaching Of Democracy In Schools', Qualifications and Curriculum Authority, 1998

[41] 'It's Like That', The Prince's Trust, January 2001

[42] 'Outside, Looking In', The Children's Society, March 2001

[43] Gillick v West Norfolk and Wisbech AHA, 1986

[44] *Prospect*, June 2001

[45] Eliot G 'Mill On The Floss', p. 145

Into Adulthood

Dr John Coleman

What is adulthood?

This is the question most young people would like an answer to, and yet it is unlikely that they would get the same answer from a parent, a teacher, a policeman, or a politician. The fact is that there are many different answers to the question, and we could suggest one which is based on biology, one based on the law (although even that would be complex), or one based on family practice and circumstances. One of the key issues for a young person centres around when they will be considered to be grown up. But how can this be answered? Is a 14 year-old girl who is pregnant an adult? Is a 15 year-old who is working on a neighbour's farm and earning £30 a day an adult? Is a young woman of 16 who is living in a squat in King's Cross and working as a prostitute an adult? It is unlikely that the reader will say yes to any of these, yet they raise questions about how we define this state of adulthood. Does it have to do with economic independence? Does it have to do with sexual maturity? Does it have to do with living circumstances? Or is the state of adulthood defined by law, having to do with voting age or something similar?

The reality is that adulthood cannot be defined in one dimension only. There are different strands that go to make up the adult state, and these will include economic factors, household and family formation, chronological age, sexual maturity, legal status, and so on. This may be difficult for a young person to accept, but the concept of adulthood is today too complex to be encompassed in only one dimension. It is also important to note that the transition from one stage to another is not necessarily clear-cut, and for many there will be a stage of semi-independence, or semi-autonomy. Here the young person may have moved away from home but still be dependent on the family for financial assistance. Alternatively, the young person may have become a parent themselves, and yet still be living in the family home. These and many other combinations of circumstances are part of the route taken by individuals as they seek to reach full adult status.[1]

In thinking about this issue it is clearly important to recognise the part the law plays in defining adulthood. As many authors have pointed out[2], the law, as it stands at present in the UK, is far from satisfactory, and there is much work to be done in this arena. Today the age of consent for both heterosexual and homosexual relationships is set at 16, whilst what is known as the age of majority is set at 18. In addition, one cannot drive a car until 17, yet one can get married at 16, so long as parental consent has been obtained. The age of criminal responsibility is currently 10 in England and Wales, yet the age at which the adult minimum wage rate begins is 22. Thus, it can be seen that there is wide variability in legal definitions of adult status. A further issue arises in relation to questions of medical confidentiality. Medical practitioners are put in the position where they have to determine whether an individual under the age of 16 is mature enough to take a decision concerning their health without the knowledge or agreement of the parents. If the medical practitioner so determines, then it is possible that a 14 or 15 year-old is treated as an adult in the health context, thus leading to further uncertainty about the nature of adult status.

In thinking about adulthood, it is also important to reflect on the fact that social and historical change have had an impact on how we define this stage of human development.[3] A wide variety of factors have influenced the way we construe childhood and adolescence, and these changes in perception have in turn led to a shifting view of adulthood. It is generally acknowledged that adolescence is starting earlier and ending later. This in turn means a longer transition or 'in-between' period between childhood and adulthood. Such an extended transition has inevitably given rise to even further confusion about appropriate definitions of adulthood.

How has this happened? In the first place, many believe that puberty is now starting earlier, possibly well before the teenage years arrive. While the evidence for this remains debatable, nonetheless there is little doubt that adolescent social behaviour is to be seen in the playground before children make the transfer from primary to secondary school.

Experiences in secondary school too have changed, for there is today a far greater emphasis on performance and on examinations. This is partly to do with the competition in the labour market which will be discussed below, and partly to do with a growing emphasis on league tables and comparisons between schools. The introduction of a national curriculum has also led to a standardisation of education, and to a lack of flexibility in meeting the needs of individual pupils. Many have suffered as a result of such policies, especially those who are less able academically. For these young people finding a role in the school setting is problematic, leading to pessimism and disaffection regarding the possibilities of adulthood.

In addition to this, it is undoubtedly true to say that, for the older adolescent, it is taking longer to reach economic independence today than 20 years ago. I shall have more to say about this in the next section, but, for the moment, we can note that few now go into work at 16. Most young people continue in some form of education or training until at least 18, and many continue in this situation into their twenties. If adolescence is extended at both ends then inevitably the attainment of adulthood becomes more problematic.

Into the labour market

Entry into the labour market at the beginning of the 21st century is more difficult than it was during the latter part of the last century. As I have just noted, it takes longer, there is more uncertainty and less security in employment, and particular groups suffer especial disadvantage. The comments I am about to make concerning the altered labour market apply to the UK, but it is important to remember that all Western countries have experienced similar conditions during the last couple of decades. A dramatic rise in unemployment occurred in the late 1970s and early 1980s. This trend was more apparent among young workers than among any other group, to the extent that unemployment rates for young men between the ages of 16 and 24 in the UK increased from 5% to 25% in the decade 1974-1984. Similar, but less marked, increases were also seen for young women. In essence, the overall size of the labour market reduced in this period, and those in the younger age groups were vulnerable to market forces. The historical shift can clearly be seen by looking at the numbers of young people in employment during this period. In the years 1984-1999 the numbers of individuals aged 16-24 in the labour market shrunk by nearly 35%, as shown in Figure 1.

FIGURE 1
Numbers of 16-24 year-olds in the labour force, in the UK, 1984-1999.

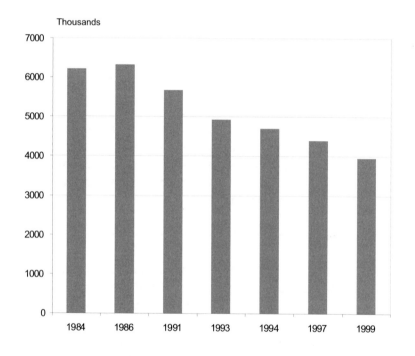

Source: Social Trends 26 and 30. The Stationery Office. 1996 and 2000.

Changes such as these have a wide range of implications. In the first place, the onus has been on government to introduce a number of job training and job preparation schemes to assist young people into employment. These schemes have had the secondary benefit of ensuring that entry into the labour market is delayed, thus reducing the numbers who might appear in unemployment statistics. The rigorous demands of the New Deal have put additional pressure on less able young people, pushing them even more forcefully into some type of training between the ages of 16 and 18.

A second implication is that the further and higher education sector has grown enormously.[4] Almost all young people continue in some form of education after compulsory school leaving age, and significant numbers go on to higher education after the age of 18. In 2001 roughly 33% of this age group are in higher education, and it is the government's objective that this figure reaches as high as 50% of the age group in the next ten years. This development has not only led to a postponement of employment, and a reduction of those in late adolescence and early adulthood who are participants in the labour market, but it has also had major financial implications for families and for the state. The argument over student loans reflects very clearly the impossible position of government here. The labour market has shrunk, so that fewer young people can be employed in stable long-term jobs. It is essential that those in the 16-25 year age group are occupied. However, if they are not in work then there is a huge financial burden to be carried by someone, and it is not surprising that the state wishes to avoid such an obligation.

While it is clear that entry into the labour market has become more difficult for this age group, this is not the only change that is of relevance to young adults. Another important social trend has to do with the composition of the work force. Since 1950 in Britain the manufacturing sector has reduced from approximately 35% of the total labour market to 16%, whereas the service sector has increased from 8% to 23%. These shifts have meant that young men have lost traditional sources of employment, whilst young women have gained new opportunities for work. In addition to this, social disadvantage impacts on employment patterns and prospects. One illustration of this is that young people from ethnic minority backgrounds are significantly more likely to be unemployed than white young people. This dramatic difference is illustrated in Figure 2.

FIGURE 2
Unemployment rates for 18-24 year-olds, by
ethnic group in the UK, 1999

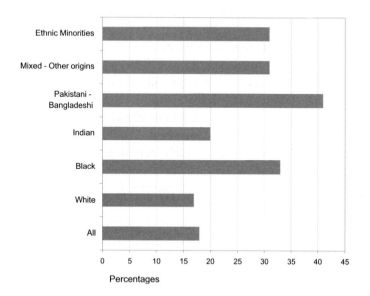

Source: Labour Force Statistics, May 2000. The
Stationery Office

Up to this point we have been discussing the labour market in terms of jobs that are full-time, provide a degree of stability, and offer a salary on which it is possible to live independently. However, the labour market also offers a completely different type of work opportunity, namely part-time, low paid jobs suitable for young people from 10 and 11 upwards. There has recently been a growing level of concern about this type of labour market, primarily because more and more young people are involved in it, and because of the impact such work has on other aspects of the lives of these adolescents. Figures derived from a survey carried out by the TUC in 2001 show that 35 % of 11-16 year-olds have part-time jobs, many of them paid very poorly indeed. A significant number of children who work in these jobs suffer pressure to miss school when the employer requires, and many of them experience a conflict between school work and the demands of this part-time employment.

A similar situation exists for those who are students in higher and further education. Because of the limited or non-existent financial support available to such students, and because often student loans or family support are insufficient to meet living requirements, students find themselves having to work to make ends meet. While there has been little research into this problem, anecdotal evidence shows that the majority of students in Britain are now taking part-time casual work, inevitably affecting their performance and often their health. Clearly work experience during adolescence and early adulthood can provide positive benefits, but these have got to be weighed against the need to study and achieve the necessary qualifications at the end of education or training. More research is needed to ensure that part-time work for students does not prove an obstacle to obtaining stable long-term employment.

The changing labour market has significant implications for our understanding of adulthood. Perhaps most important of all is the fact that delayed entry into work means delayed achievement of financial independence. Since such independence is a tangible sign of adulthood, the prolongation of dependence has serious consequences both for the family and for the personal development of the individual. In addition, a shrinking labour market means more competition for jobs, thus making qualifications even more important. This in turn puts greater pressure on individuals in relation to examinations and achievements in education, possibly causing increased levels of stress. Since, in some senses, young people reach maturity even earlier today (as for example in their sexual development) the question has to be asked: how do individuals express their autonomy and sense of individuality if they cannot become fully independent through work? We will return to this question in the final section of the chapter.

Changing family structures

There is no doubt that alterations in the structure of the family have had almost as much impact on young people and their entry into adulthood as have the changes in the labour market. As is well known, the divorce rate in Western countries increased steadily during the 1970s and 1980s. In the 1990s the divorce rate levelled out, but other changes have become apparent, in particular the fact that more and more children are being born outside marriage. It is among young adults that this trend is most marked, and recent evidence shows that in Britain more than three quarters of children born to parents under 20 are born outside marriage. Thus, the increase in the numbers of families headed by a lone parent is not only a result of divorce, but also stems from changes in attitudes to marriage and partnership in relation to child-bearing. This historical trend is illustrated by figures shown in Figure 3.

FIGURE 3
Births outside marriage, England and Wales, 1971 -1999

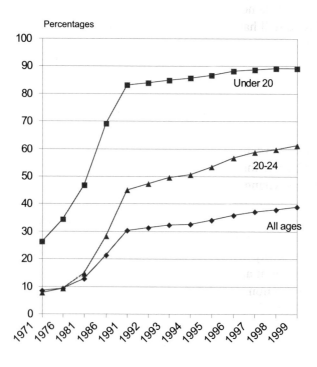

Source: Population Trends, 100. Summer 2000. Office for National Statistics.

An equally important trend is the number of young people growing towards adulthood who experience the break-up of their parents' marriages. Today, in some European countries, nearly one in four 16 year-olds live in a family where there has been a divorce. In the United States the figure is closer to one in three. Such changes in family structure have repercussions in a number of areas. The most obvious of these repercussions is that a significant proportion of children and adolescents will have had to cope with family reorganisation, and with the loss of one parent. Possible consequences of this may include greater stress and less support from the immediate family.

Young people are experiencing a variety of family arrangements, including step-families, live-in partners, remarriage, and so on. Furthermore, it is not just the individuals whose parents divorce who are influenced by these new family forms. In practice everyone is affected, since everyone will have a friend, neighbour or relative in whose family there has been a divorce or some form of rearrangement of living circumstances. Our attitudes to marriage are changing, and our experiences now encompass a much wider range of family types than was the case in previous decades.

Apart from the stress caused by family reconstitution, changing family structures have two other implications for young people. In the first place, it is probable that values and beliefs about marriage and the family are shifting as young people grow up in families that are, relatively speaking, less stable than was the case for their own mothers and fathers. While we still do not know for certain how these experiences affect the individual's own passage towards adulthood, it seems highly likely that the lack of stability will impact on the nature of partnerships in the future. At present, it appears that marriage is still highly valued, but that there is more caution about this state. Individuals now marry later, and there is more fluidity in personal relationships in late adolescence and early adulthood. The fact that so many children are now being born outside marriage supports this conclusion.

The second implication of changing family structures is that the parenting of teenagers is more problematic. We live in a world where there is already considerable uncertainty about what constitutes effective parenting for an adolescent in normal circumstances. However, when we have to grapple with questions concerning the parenting roles of lone parents, step-parents, and new partners, not to mention the roles of the divorced or separated parents living apart from the children, then clearly there are additional challenges and difficulties to be faced. Uncertainty about parenting practices is not good for teenagers or parents, especially since adolescence is the time, more than any other in the life of a family, when parenting confidence is at a premium. As remarriage and family reorganisation become more common it is essential that we give greater consideration to the ways in which young adults are being affected by changing family structures.

Sexual development

Of all the areas of adolescent development which cause difficulty for the adult world, teenage sexuality is pre-eminent. In a remarkable way the sexual maturity of our children appears to represent to parents and other adults an enormous challenge. Above all, it is symbolic of the moment when we finally lose control over our sons and daughters, and there is little doubt that the key issue between adults and young people is to do with power and control. Also, of course, becoming sexually active represents the attainment of adult status in a way which no other behaviour can do. Indeed, it could be argued that to commence a sexual relationship is even more symbolic of maturity than to become financially independent. Another important factor here is that adult sexual behaviour has altered so much in the last four decades. This, I would argue, has contributed greatly to the muddle and confusion in adult minds over how to treat adolescent sexuality.

Before we consider the implications of teenage sexual behaviour for our consideration of adulthood, let us look at what we know about young people in this regard. While many people still view the 1960s as the most permissive decade of the 20th century, the evidence would appear to contradict that, certainly in respect of adolescent sexual behaviour. It should be noted that we are handicapped to some extent by the fact that there have been so few studies of this behaviour, and this is particularly true of sexual behaviour under the age of 16. Nonetheless, the evidence we do have all points to a gradual increase in sexual behaviour among young people, with teenagers becoming sexually active at younger ages today than in previous decades. To give one example, results from a major study published in 2001[5] indicate that in the UK approximately 25% of young women and 28% of young men report having had sex before reaching the age of 16. These are considerably higher numbers than have been found in studies of the 1980s.

Another associated issue, and one which has aroused considerable public interest, is the question of whether puberty is getting earlier. This is obviously important for a number of reasons, not least because, if children are reaching sexual maturity at an ever earlier age, it is reasonable to conclude that they are likely to become sexually active at ever earlier ages. However, the scientific facts are hard to establish, and the subject remains shrouded in controversy. Whilst teachers report more girls starting their periods in primary school today than was the case ten or twenty years ago, there has been only limited research which throws light on this question. Studies in the USA do seem to support the notion of, at least, the commencement of puberty becoming earlier, but we still lack European data on this topic.[6] However, it is clearly important to establish the truth of the matter. If puberty is starting earlier, then sex education strategies in school need to take this into account. Even more important, however, is the impact on changing sexual behaviour. If we can expect more sexual behaviour from those in early adolescence then appropriate sexual health services and contraceptive advice become especially important if we are to avoid ever higher levels of teenage pregnancy.

Teenage pregnancy is, of course, the most tangible manifestation of sexual behaviour during adolescence. It is a focus for adult anxieties, and has led to a range of government initiatives aimed at reducing rates of pregnancy in this age group. The most recent of these in the UK was the establishment of the Teenage Pregnancy Unit within the Department of Health, the objective of which is to alter attitudes, improve services and develop new strategies for the prevention of pregnancy. Such an initiative is given added impetus by the oft-quoted fact that Britain has the highest rate of teenage pregnancy among member countries of the European Union.

It is of interest to note that, as can be seen from the figures illustrated in Figure 4, rates of conception for the under-16s in England and Wales have not changed very much in the last three decades. Thus, it may seem as if public hysteria over rates of teenage pregnancy is rather misplaced. However, this picture has to be set against the fact that, in almost all European countries, rates have come down substantially in the last 20 years. Britain is the only country which has not shown a decline in rates of teenage pregnancy, thereby raising a host of questions about our sex education strategy, our sexual health services for young people, and our attitudes to teenage sex.

FIGURE 4

Conception rates in England and Wales, 13-15 year-olds, 1969-1998

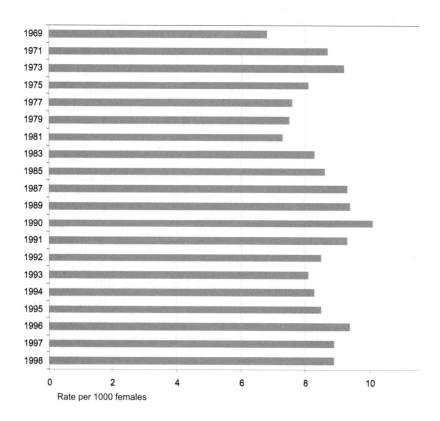

Source: Population Trends, Spring 2000. Office for National Statistics.

As we noted above, for a young person to become sexually active is one way, perhaps the easiest way, in which to achieve something which symbolises adult status. In addition this is an area of behaviour over which adults have little control. However much a parent would wish to be able to prevent, or even delay, the start of a sexual relationship by a teenage son or daughter, there is little a mother or father can do in the face of a determined adolescent. Where other forms of autonomy or independence are difficult or impossible to attain, it may be in the sexual arena that young people find it easiest to express their need to be 'grown up'. If we wish to address the issues surrounding teenage sexuality, we need not only to provide better education and improved services, but also to recognise and address the individual young person's need for autonomy and a recognized status in society.

Boys and girls are different

In relation to gender there has been an important shift in public attitudes over the last thirty years. Whilst in the 1970s and 1980s the needs of girls and young women were high on the policy and research agendas, this situation has now changed markedly, with much more concern being expressed about boys and young men.[7] High rates of male youth crime and school exclusions have led to increasing concern over 'the problem with boys'. Young men, especially under-achieving young men, are portrayed as posing a problem for society. This has been linked to a range of worries about fathering, and about the impact on male children of the absentee father, either due to long hours at work, or to divorce and family breakdown. An even more recent shift has been towards the depiction of young men as victims. This notion has stemmed from the publicity given to high rates of suicide among young men, as well as to problems of under-achievement, social exclusion and unemployment.

Let us look first at education. Undoubtedly the most important fact here is the improved performance of girls at GCSE level during the 1990s. While the performance of boys has also improved, it has not kept pace with the improvements being demonstrated year on year by young women at age 16. It is also of interest to note that subject choice is gendered. Girls do better in subjects such as English, maths, the sciences, and languages. Boys do better in business studies, IT and geography. This gender gap has been consistent for many years. Not surprisingly, there has been considerable debate over the reasons for the gender differences in performance at GCSE level. Some have argued that the format of the examination is favourable to a female approach to learning. However, we should also recognise that changing patterns of work, as well as greater employment opportunities for females, both of which have been referred to earlier, have had an impact on the motivation of girls and young women.

Turning now to the picture for those who have left school, gender differences continue to be noticeable. In broad terms, more young women stay on in education after the age of 16, whilst more young men go into occupational schemes or job training. As far as choice of subjects and types of employment are concerned, these are even more closely linked with gender than is subject choice in the school years. Of those intending to choose some form of managerial/professional career, 75% are male, compared with 25% of young women. In contrast, 77% of those intending to choose 'personal services' careers are female, and only 23% male. This diversity reflects a continuing gender gap in terms of perceptions of opportunity and appropriateness of different careers for the two genders.

'A' level choices also show a strong gender disparity. English, history, biology and languages are all more heavily subscribed by young women, whilst maths, physics and technology are selected more by young men. These choices are consistent with the types of career choice suggested above. It is also worth noting that more young men than young women in the 16 to 18 year age group are registered unemployed. However, young women who are outside employment, education or training, often have responsibilities as carers, and thus they constitute a hidden group who are not part of any statistics. Undoubtedly, young people's experiences during this stage of their lives are critical for the way they are able to take on their adult roles. It is likely that inequality of opportunity works against both young men and young women at this time, but in different ways. Young women from poorer backgrounds are more likely to have family responsibilities, whilst young men who are less able face a shrinking labour market.

In thinking about gender, one other area worth mentioning is that of health and health-related behaviour. Recent reviews have indicated that, contrary to the popular belief that the adolescent years are the most healthy, in fact, many young people suffer serious health problems.[8] In addition, there are numerous issues around access to health services, and the difficulties that some young people face in this respect. Research indicates that both young women and young men can be vulnerable to health problems, but that vulnerability operates differently depending on gender. In the first place mortality rates in this age group (16-24 year-olds) are strikingly higher for males than for females, in the ratio of 3:1. This is primarily because of the incidence of accidents and suicide, a topic to which we shall return to below. Males are more likely to drink heavily, whilst girls are more likely to be smokers. Females over the age of 17 are more likely to visit the GP than males, and in general it does appear that females are more able to access services than males. There are many possible reasons for the gender differences in accessing services. The most likely are disparities in communication skills, varying attitudes to health among young women and young men, and services structured to appeal more to women than to men.

Finally, gender differences are particularly apparent in the arena of sexual health. In spite of the notion of 'girl power' young women still find it difficult to say no to sex, and to negotiate the use of contraception. Confidentiality remains an issue for young people when they do use services, and many girls under the age of 16 are uncertain of their rights in relation to seeking help and advice without their parents being informed. The situation for young men appears to be no easier. They continue to feel pressured to be sexually active, and they find it hard to access services, to admit inexperience, and to talk about their emotions where intimate relationships are concerned. One issue of note, especially in relation to gender, is the recent increase in the incidence of sexually transmitted infections among young adults. Not only is the increase itself of concern, but the rates for such things as chlamydia and genital warts are between 5 and 10 times higher for young women than for young men. There are a number of possible reasons for this difference, including vulnerability to particular types of sexually transmitted infection, and differing attitudes among males and females towards seeking health care. This poses a significant challenge for intervention as well as for health promotion, and underlines the necessity of having individual services and programmes tailored for young men and young women.

We can conclude that males and females progress towards adulthood in somewhat different ways. Gender differences remain striking across a range of domains in this age group, as is illustrated by some of the areas we have discussed above. Of all the issues mentioned perhaps the one that should give us most concern is the remarkable evidence of stereotyped career choices. When there is continual discussion about women's rights, and about equal opportunities in society, it is a sobering thought that among those who will be adults in the coming decades, there is still incontrovertible evidence of a gendered perception of male and female occupational roles. There is a lot of work to be done if this gender divide is to be addressed in the future.

Vulnerability in the transition to adulthood

There is a cogent argument to be advanced that the transition to adulthood is more problematic at the beginning of the 21st century than it has been since the early years of the 20th century. A variety of factors contribute to this, most especially delayed entry into the labour market, changing family structures, and a scarcity of resources, both human and financial, available to those in the 16-24 year age range. We will return to this argument in the final section of the chapter, and consider its wider implications for society. For the present, however, I wish to focus on those who are unusually vulnerable during this stage of their lives. While everyone may experience a series of challenges and obstacles during this period, there are some who deserve special attention, and here I will concentrate on those with mental health problems, and those who have been identified as being at risk of social exclusion.

I have already mentioned high rates of suicide among young men in this age group. It is particularly striking that suicide rates are three to four times higher in males than in females. While rates for young women in the UK have remained stable at around four per 100,000, rates for young men between the ages of 16 and 24 have risen as high as 17 per 100,000 in the late 1980s and 1990s.[9] This is a very worrying trend, with no simple explanation. Possible factors include a worsening economic situation, increased use of alcohol and drugs, greater availability of weapons, and poor communication skills among young men with respect to emotional problems. However, it should also be pointed out that there are significant regional variations. At present, rates are highest in Scotland, and in 1997 they reached a level of 30 young men per 100,000 taking their lives through suicide. Another way to look at these figures is to note that in the UK as a whole, a total of 571 young men died as a result of suicide in the year 1998: a shocking figure, and one which demands urgent public debate.

Three possible reasons are suggested for these high figures. In the first place, harsh economic conditions affect young men in particular, leaving them with little hope for the future. In addition, young men are more likely than young women to be involved in drug abuse, a significant contributory factor in suicide. Thirdly, we have already noted the possibility that young men find it hard to access services and to communicate their emotional distress.

While the spotlight has been focussed on young men in relation to completed suicides, this should not obscure the need to pay attention also to the problem of attempted suicide. Although figures are more difficult to obtain, the best research we have indicates that the gender ratio is almost exactly reversed here, with approximately four young women attempting suicide for every young man doing so. National figures are not available, but a team in Oxford led by Professor Keith Hawton estimates that as many as 20,000 young people are likely to be referred to hospital every year because of an episode of attempted suicide.

Of course, there are many other reflections of mental health problems, apart from the extreme forms discussed so far. Depression, eating disorders, being the victim of bullying, and other psychiatric disorders all cause untold distress, and yet here again we have only limited knowledge of the scale of the problem. An important study[10] appeared in 2000, the first to document the extent of mental health difficulties among young people in England, Scotland and Wales. This study showed that approximately 12% of all young people suffer from some form of serious mental distress during their adolescence. Young women are more likely to experience neurotic disorders, while young men are more likely to be classified as having conduct disorders.

As we have noted, there are some groups of young people who may be considered to be particularly vulnerable. Those from minority ethnic communities are one group where it is possible that there are higher rates of mental health problems. One example of this is the markedly higher rate of deliberate self-harm among South Asian young women. Further light has been shed on this issue by the study mentioned above. From this it appears that young black people suffer significantly higher rates of mental health problems than young white people. More research is urgently needed in this field to assist in the appropriate delivery of services. Another group, about which concern is frequently expressed, is those young people looked after by local authorities. Studies that have been carried out in the 1990s have shown extremely high rates of disorder among this group, a fact which has led to the establishment of 'Quality Protects', a government initiative designed to improve services for young people who are in care. It is still too early to be able to tell how this will impact on the lives of these young people, but at least the problem is now recognized at the policy level.

Turning now to the notion of social exclusion, it should be noted that much recent thinking about youth in Britain has included some ideas about marginality and alienation. Indeed, by establishing the Social Exclusion Unit in 1997, the Labour government confirmed the importance of such an idea. Ten years ago the debate centred around a related but different concept, that of an 'underclass'. Much was written pointing out the likelihood that in our country there appeared to be a growing threat to social cohesion from a group of young men who were permanently marginalised, living outside the normal social conventions, living a life of crime and anarchy.

This concept had a number of different themes associated with it. On the one hand, there was a general belief that crime and disorder was on the increase. High profile incidents such as riots in inner city estates, gave credence to this view. On the other hand, there was concern about those who were out of work, and who seemed unwilling to become involved in training schemes or other employment opportunities. This concern was linked with the decline of jobs in manufacturing industry, a point noted earlier. In addition to all this there was a third theme which added fuel to the anxiety, namely a concern about masculinity in our culture. It was pointed out that young men most often involved in crime came from families where fathers were absent. Thus lone mothers, inadequate fathers, and the lack of what were called positive role models for young men, all became targets for the angst of politicians and the media.

The more thoughtful commentators[11] were able to show that young men growing up in poverty and deprivation were unlikely to be a serious threat to our society. Such young people were most often individuals who were marginalised as a result of forces beyond their control, lacking the resources or the skills to undermine the country's institutions. Growing up in dysfunctional families, in poor neighbourhoods, often being unable to engage with school, and having limited opportunities for stable employment, these young men were victims of circumstance rather than agents of social disorder. As the political climate has changed, a growing interest in social exclusion has become evident. Today, a more rational approach is being taken to the problems of those who experience difficulty during late adolescence and early adulthood.

In considering social exclusion, it remains to emphasise the fact that there are some especially vulnerable groups of young people in our society. There is no doubt that those from some ethnic minorities fall into this category. We noted earlier their difficulties in entering employment. Another group is those who leave the care of the local authority at the age of 16 or 18. Research shows that over 40% of those in custody or secure accommodation have been in care. More than one third of young women leaving care become pregnant within the first 12 months. Very few have any educational attainments, and the great majority of homeless young people are those who have been looked after by local authorities. Other vulnerable groups include those who fail to engage in any form of education or training post-16. The New Deal may have an impact on this group, but it is still too early to tell whether there will be a substantial reduction in the numbers falling into this category in the next few years. Finally, the group with special needs, and those with disabilities are also especially vulnerable. For such young people their transition to adulthood may be fraught, not only with the obstacles already noted, but also with a range of other hurdles which we as a society still do too little to address.

Making the transition easier -
the role of the family and of the state

I have noted a number of times in the course of this chapter my belief that the transition to adulthood in western societies has become more problematic during the last few decades. As I have specified, contributory factors include the changing nature of the labour market, the alterations in family structures, the competition for resources between older and younger groups in the population, and the continuing difficulty that adults seem to find in treating adolescents as 'trainee adults' rather than as threatening trouble-makers. In this concluding section I wish to explore how both the family and the state could contribute to making the transition an easier and more fruitful process.

Looking first at the family, it is necessary to point out that all research underlines the key place occupied by the family as a support for young people as they make the transition to adulthood. This is particularly pertinent in situations of difficulty and uncertainty. The family, even if it is an unsatisfactory family, is the only setting in which the young person can obtain the recognition and endorsement that is so necessary for any individual making key life choices. For this reason the structure and functioning of the family assumes paramount importance during this stage, and yet there remain major questions in relation to the role of parents for young people between the ages of 16 and 24.

For both adults and young people the ideal family during this stage is one which is described as a democracy. Decisions should be taken, and power shared, on an equal basis, with all parties feeling that their needs and concerns are taken into account. In practice this is rarely the case. While both parents and adolescents pay lip service to this notion of equality, in fact parents frequently attempt to exercise control over the lives of their sons and daughters, and young people find ways of keeping crucial information to themselves, thereby retaining some element of autonomy from their parents.

There is, throughout society, a degree of uncertainty over the rights and responsibilities of parents during this stage of life. On the one hand, governments of all colours during the last 20 years have emphasised the responsibilities of parents, and yet in the real world it is exceptionally hard for parents to carry out these responsibilities if the young person is unwilling to accept parental control. This situation is complicated by the continuing financial responsibilities of parents. Is it right that mothers and fathers have to go on finding money for their 18 or 19 year-old, while at the same time recognising that this individual is very unlikely to accept guidance or direction? There is no doubt that this continuing drain on the family can cause serious strain. In addition, the new type of relationship demanded of parents and young people as a result of continuing financial dependency raises a set of new questions about the rights of each party.

One of the central factors which contributes to the key role played by the family is the lack of clarity today in the routes to adulthood[12]. The more uncertainty young people experience, the more they depend on their primary support network. Recent research highlights the fact that there are fewer and fewer defined pathways for young people during the transition to adulthood. Very large numbers experience a situation where they have to invent the best route for themselves, depending on local circumstance. In such situations support from adults becomes critical. The state has shown little inclination to recognise this, and appears to be caught in a trap of its own making. Government is encouraging more and more young people into further and higher education, without tackling the concomitant problems of finance for such students and the creation of suitable employment at the end of long periods of education.

In the recent review of youth policy in the UK referred to above[13], it was noted that there are a range of inconsistencies in this field. Transitions and status shifts are often defined by chronological age, and yet it is clear that this is far from the most appropriate means to define such things. The state places much emphasis on citizenship, and yet there are very few opportunities for young people to exercise real power in their lives. Most important of all, there are a range of policies treating young people as less economically independent than adults, and yet at the same time the state seems unwilling to debate or think seriously about how the period of economic dependence will be managed. It is obvious that the burden will fall on the family, and yet this is not properly acknowledged. Those families taking on this burden suffer in a variety of ways, while those young people without families also suffer during this transition. Circumstances have changed out of all recognition for young people over the last 20 years, and it is high time the state developed policies that acknowledged these changes, and provided appropriate support for the families of young people as they struggle to achieve adulthood.

At the very minimum government should think in practical terms about how initiatives that reflect a genuine commitment to joined-up action can be put into place. While there has been much talk about integration between central and local government, between the statutory and voluntary sectors, and between different government departments, there has been too little evidence to show that such integration is actually taking place. Further, there needs to be a greater focus on the adolescent age group, and, in particular on the needs of those between the ages of 16 and 21. The government's Children and Young People's Unit is admirable in its intentions, but its brief (ages 0-19) is too broad to make any real difference to the older groups. Changed thinking in the financial sphere is also necessary. The initiative involving Education Maintenance Grants - enabling poor students to stay on in education after the age of 16 - is an important development, but needs to be extended to cover the whole country. It could also be offered to a wider range of students. Finally, the funding of higher education also urgently needs a new and imaginative approach. A more coherent and equitable system is necessary so that students are encouraged rather than discouraged into education after the age of 18. As has been argued in this chapter, entry into adulthood is problematic for many in our society. For the health of society government policy must address the more pressing needs of this age group.

---

[1] Coleman J and Hendry L 'The nature of adolescence' 3rd Edn., Routledge, London, 1999

[2] For example Jones G and Bell R 'Balancing acts: youth, parenting and public policy' Joseph Rowntree Foundation, York, 2000

[3] Coleman J and Hendry L 'The nature of adolescence' 3rd Edn., Routledge, London, 1999

[4] Coleman J and Schofield J 'Key data on adolescence' The Trust for the Study of Adolescence, Brighton, 2001

[5] Wellings K et.al. 'Sexual behaviour in Britain: early heterosexual experience' The Lancet, 358, 2001, pp. 1843-1850

[6] Coleman J and Hendry L 'The nature of adolescence' 3rd Edn., Routledge, London, 1999

[7] Dennison C and Coleman J 'Young people and gender: a review of research' The Cabinet Office, London, 2000

[8] Coleman J and Schofield J 'Key data on adolescence' The Trust for the Study of Adolescence, Brighton, 2001

[9] ibid

[10] McDonald R (ed.) 'Youth, the underclass and social exclusion' Routledge, London, 1997

[11] For example Melzer H et al. 'Mental health of children and adolescents in Great Britain' Office for National Statistics, Stationery Office, London, 2000

[12] Coles B 'Joined-up youth research: policy and practice. A new agenda for change?' Youth Work Press, Leicester, 2001

[13] ibid

Relationships
The Birth of the Liberal Family

Helen Wilkinson

This book is about the seven ages of life. But relationships are not so much a stage in one's life as the glue through which the various stages and phases of life are brought together. Birth, childhood, the transition into adulthood, into work, parenthood and retirement, death are all mediated through networks of relationships that we form - both good and bad. Ultimately, of course, it is relationships which produce the ties that bind, relationships that create and foster the kinship networks and the reciprocity and mutual obligation between lovers, between parents and children and across the generations which last a lifetime. It is through the prism of loving relationships that we judge so much about our lives. For society, too, it is the relationships and family ties that we form which generate social capital and create long term social cohesion. This chapter is about the relationships that we forge through the life-cycle - how these have changed and continue to evolve, and the challenges thrown up by these changes for liberals and for policy-makers.

Relationships over time

It is widely acknowledged that relationships and family life have changed significantly over the course of the last few generations. The most common narrative about traditional relationships is that they began with a courtship, evolved to engagement, on to marriage and then to parenthood. Intimate sexual relationships rarely took place outside of the married state, and parenthood and marriage were symbiotic. Marriage breakdown, adultery and infidelity were frowned upon and relatively rare. The processes of relationship formation and the various stages that relationships moved through were relatively linear and predictable. And there was not a lot of choice about it.

To anyone born in the 1960s or beyond - whom I have called 'freedom's children' - such a narrative about relationships and family life is oddly out of kilter with the way they live their lives, or indeed observed the lives of their parents' generation. There is a straightforward sociological reason for this. The 1960s stand as an important fault line in relationships and family life. It is since the 1960s that the divorce rate began to increase exponentially; since the 1960s that sex before marriage became commonplace; that marriage was challenged by cohabitation, both as a stage before marriage and increasingly as a replacement for it. And since the 1960s the umbilical link between marriage and parenthood has been cut with parenthood existing outside of the married state as well as within it. Ponder on these trends:

- Declining marriage

  Marriage as an institution is in decline. The rate of first marriage has been steadily falling over the last thirty years. Between 1970 and 1999 the number of first marriages taking place in the UK has halved.[1] Couples are increasingly choosing to defer marriage, with the average age for first-time brides up from 25 to 28 and for first-time grooms up from 27 to 30 in the ten years between 1989 and 1999.[2]

- Rise of cohabitation

  This trend has seen an accompanying rise in rates of cohabitation. In 1996 there were just over 1.5 million cohabiting couples in England and Wales, representing around one sixth of the adult non-married population, and this number is predicted to double within twenty years.[3]

  This pattern is being driven by a younger generation in their twenties and thirties. Whilst marriage was still the dominant way of entering a partnership for women born in the 1950s and early 60s, subsequent generations of women have increasingly chosen to cohabit before marriage.[4] In addition, little more than half of these younger women will have gone on to marry, suggesting that for growing numbers cohabitation has come to represent a more permanent long-term relationship model.[5] This is perhaps reflected in the manner in which more and more couples are choosing to start families without feeling the need to get married first. The number of births taking place out of wedlock has increased rapidly since the late 1970s, accounting for nearly two fifths of all births by 1999, of which 60% were jointly registered by parents living at the same address.[6]

• Relationship breakdown

The attractions of marriage as a provider of stability have been challenged by rising levels of relationship breakdown. The divorce rate rose rapidly in the late 1960s and 70s, reaching a peak in 1993. Although there is some evidence to suggest that the divorce rate is now on its way down, with the most recent statistics showing the lowest number of annual divorces since 1979[7], these figures do not reflect the additional incidence of breakdown amongst the growing numbers of cohabiting couples, or separations between still married spouses. And the divorce rate has actually risen amongst those married for the second or subsequent time.[8]

• Single life

It is unsurprising, therefore, to find that the proportion of people choosing to live the single life or finding themselves single over the life course has increased, in sharp contrast to earlier generations. Figures show that 14% of all households in Spring 2000 were comprised of individuals of below retirement age living alone. This represents more than double the proportion in 1971.[9] The number of single-member households containing women under the age of 65 has almost doubled, whilst amongst men of the same age the increase is roughly three-fold, with this group projected soon to become the largest category of single-member households in Britain.[10]

We are not alone in experiencing these patterns in the UK. Declining marriage rates are an international phenomenon, having fallen on average by 20% since 1965 in Northern and Western Europe.[11]

• Modern-day intimacy

We should be wary of conflating these linear trends with the demise of family life. Family life is much more organic than linear trends suggest. Today's lone parent is tomorrow's reconstituted family. The same people who marry, divorce and become single, rarely remain so throughout their life. They go on to form new relationships, new commitments, and these build on the family commitments they already have. One study of family change in the 1990s for example found that in a single year, 3% of children experienced parental separation, but 2.5% saw the arrival of a step parent or the return of a natural parent. Families are reforming, and reconstituting all the time.

One thing, however, can be said for certain. These trends illustrate how marriage is now but one lifestyle choice of many and how the character of marriage and its meaning is changing. Modern day relationships are no longer characterised by an easily identified structure, but more by diversity and an ever expanding range of personal choices. In the 1960's people's values started to change - a new morality began to hold sway which placed a higher value on individual happiness and emotional fulfilment. One consequence is that it broke down many of the rigid ethical codes and social taboos of the past. As attitudes towards sexuality and non-nuclear family forms became more relaxed, especially amongst the post-war generation, marriage has had to work harder for its status as the moral cornerstone of society and family life.[12] At the same time people began to experiment with other ways of living and loving, and even the heterosexual norm came under challenge. Gay relationships have increasingly come out of the closet and 'the love that dare not speak its name' has a generation on become more widely accepted still.

The birth of the liberal family

Many of the changes described above indicate a liberalisation of relationships and family life, a retreat from tradition and an embrace of greater individual freedom and autonomy. In short, we are witnessing the birth of the liberal family.

For liberals, these changes are on balance positive, and even so called 'negative' trends, such as the escalating divorce rate, can be seen not so much as a sign that society is fraying at the edges but as an indicator of progress, as Theodore Zeldin, author of an Intimate History of Humanity, has argued. People no longer prepared to tolerate loveless marriages may find through divorce a renewed chance of fulfilment and happiness.

There are many ways in which this increasing liberalism manifests. After all, the principles and values of liberalism involve democratic values, an acceptance and celebration of diversity and difference, a commitment to freedom and autonomy, an embrace of modernity and, perhaps most important of all, the concept of choice.

This idea of the 'liberal family' appears to be firmly grounded in reality, as a number of studies tracking social change have shown.[13] Anthony Giddens, for instance, has described the emergence of the democratic family, where roles are negotiated and the decision making process is open and collaborative.

This new egalitarianism and retreat from tradition in family life are manifested in two main ways. On the one hand, there is much greater equality and openness between men and women in today's families than in the past, especially among the young,[14] and helps to explain the transition from what sociologists have described as 'marriage as an institution' to 'marriage as a relationship'.[15] The hierarchical structure and rigid role separation of the traditional model have been replaced by new values of emotional intimacy, equality, mutual affection, friendship and sexual fulfilment. Partnership has come to characterise married life for many couples today, with shared management of household finances, and greater flexibility in attitudes towards child care and household chores.[16]

On the other hand, the relationship between parent and child has also changed. Public opinion surveys confirm that the new egalitarianism isn't just affecting intimate relations between husband and wife, but is also transforming the parent-child relationship too. The talk among practitioners, as well as theorists, is of more child-centred families, where children are actively involved in the decision making process. Public opinion surveys confirm that parents increasingly feel that children should be involved in family decisions. Others have taken these arguments a step forward. Stein Ringen, in his book, *The Family In Question*[17], argues that children should be given political rights and the suffrage. Others, like myself, have argued for parents to be allotted votes by proxy to represent the interests and needs of smaller children.

The liberal ethos is also infecting attitudes to families in other ways. Younger people are taking the lead, but the new tolerance and acceptance, in some cases celebration, of diversity is widespread across the generations, with each successive generation becoming more tolerant and more accepting. This is probably the result of a growing experience of multi-culturalism and a broadening range of influences through new information technologies, most marked amongst the young and in metropolitan areas, irrespective of class background.

This tolerance extends to an acceptance - if not an outright celebration - of 'alternative' families and, in particular, those that do not fit neatly into the stereotype of traditional family life (ie stable married two parent families with 2.1 children). There is also now widespread acceptance of sex before marriage, cohabitation as a permanent state, and even parenthood outside of marriage. Today young women feel that the choices available to them are greater than ever before. Almost 90% of women aged between 18 and 34 in a recent poll either agreed or agreed strongly that there is less pressure for women today to get married and have children than a decade ago.[18]

Partly because of these broader attitudinal and demographic changes, non-traditional families - single parent households, blended and second families - are becoming more widespread and accepted, partly because of sheer force of numbers. More and more women are choosing the child-free lifestyle, and open gay relationships are becoming more common.

Increasingly people, especially in younger generations, are seeking to strike a new balance between inter-dependence and independence. For instance, couples within long-term committed relationships agree that it is important to retain and keep independent friends, and an independent social life. Moreover, sociologists have observed another trend - what has been dubbed 'intimacy at a distance' - among long-term committed partners who choose to live apart from each other but remain to all intents and purposes fully committed.

The language of choice is reverberating throughout discussions about the changing nature of family life. Traditional families, it is argued, are increasingly being replaced by 'families of choice' - families that have formed not through blood bonds or traditional ties of kinship, or notions of obligation, but which have developed out of mutual respect and affection. Gay couples have often led the way in forming these families of choice, often as a result of rejection by their biological families. A generation on, these families of choice have become commonplace among the heterosexual community. Popular culture, with TV series like *Friends* and *Cold Feet,* captures these shifts in life more generally.

The liberal family then looks set to characterise and define 21st century family life in ways that the traditional family did in the preceding two centuries. But political acceptance and endorsement of the liberal family is not a foregone conclusion: its emergence can be problematic even for liberals. Trade-offs have to be made between individual freedom and the collective public interest, especially when public resources and social cohesion are at stake. The political challenges that lie ahead in striking the right balance between liberal values and strengthening and stabilising families occupies the rest of this chapter.

The great disruption

The shift to the liberal family has not been a seamless or easy process, nor an uncontested one. On the practical level, families continue to experience huge stresses and strain. We may be coming to the end of a period of 'great disruption' along the lines described by Francis Fukuyama, but challenges remain for families on the ground. Relationships continue to break down at a rapid rate both inside and outside of marriage; more and more children are growing up in disrupted families; birth rates are in decline and society is ageing at a time when the state is trying to push back care responsibilities on to families. Moreover, the benefits of more liberal family life are not evenly spread through the population. In spite of policy initiatives to tackle social exclusion, there remain increasing divides between the haves and have-nots, and mounting child poverty. The idea of freedom in these poor communities is academic to say the least, and the gap between those that can exercise lifestyle choices and those that are denied it through poverty and social exclusion remains a major fault line threatening social cohesion at large.

To some people, especially older generations, who have grown up following the pathways laid out for them, the talk of choice and freedom appears to threaten the very notion of family itself. The long term trends suggest that we are not only living in a 'post marriage-for-life' society, in which divorce is commonplace, we are rapidly moving to a 'post marriage' one where marriage itself is increasingly redundant. Moreover, the very concept of families of choice seems to threaten the basis of family obligation through blood-ties and legal commitment for something altogether more ambiguous and ill-defined.

New Labour, new family policy

In broadening its appeal to Middle England, New Labour's policy was to steal the Conservative's rhetoric on family values and to claim it as their own. This repositioning led to the charge of social conservatism and remains a critique of New Labour's policy on the family in some quarters today. In practice, the first Labour government in a generation has been far more pragmatic when it comes to family policy than the charge of social conservatism suggests. In power they have been keen to distance themselves from any hint of 'top-down' moralising, with an emphasis on practical solutions and supporting families in all their shapes and sizes.

New Labour has sought to articulate a new set of family values to remedy the weaknesses of both the entrenched conservative and liberal positions. Conservatives have typically lamented the trends in relationships and family life, whilst liberals have tended to celebrate the greater freedoms and ignore the insecurity that have accompanied these changes. Discussions about enhancing the well-being of our children and about strengthening families themselves have all too often become lost in a fruitless tit for tat dialogue. Before we can develop a creative policy response to the formation of liberal families, we must understand the rationale for the involvement of the state in the first place.

Public policy interest

Issues of the family lie beyond individual's self interest. Liberal principles need to be measured against the collective and public policy interest. Marriage as an institution, for example, is seen to be important to society at large not least in terms of general well-being and physical health. The highest rates of GP consultation for psychiatric disorders besides the permanently sick or unemployed are amongst the divorced or separated, and men over 45 living alone have a higher mortality and higher levels of limiting long-term illness than the average for men of their age group.[19] As Glen Stanton's digest of 130 published empirical studies in this area concludes, married people generally live longer, and are more emotionally and physically healthy than the unmarried, and that includes single people and cohabitees.[20]

Similarly relationship breakdown inside, or outside of, the married state must be a concern not least because disrupted families cost the state (and taxpayers) money directly and indirectly. The state has a public interest in strengthening and stabilising families. Partly because of this, political interest in families goes much deeper. Families are the bedrock of society, the foundation of civil society, where we first learn moral values. Families generate social capital - they foster the trust and relationship skills which enable individuals to act in an inter-dependent manner. Simply put, the family is society in miniature, and it follows that family dysfunction (whether it be declining levels of trust because we do not form strong secure attachments with our lovers or with our caregivers) leads to declining social capital, and wider social dysfunction. The state and government have a role in preventing this, and therefore a balance between individual rights and those of the state and public interest needs to be found.

Given the importance of families, how can they be strengthened? Liberals need a new paradigm, a new way of thinking about families, which accepts change while preserving cohesion, and which will inform their policy decisions in the next century. What might this paradigm be?

A renewed liberalism

Historically, liberals have tended to downplay the costs of social change when it comes to relationships and family life. A revised and renewed liberalism needs to recognise that family change has brought greater freedom and autonomy but that this process has not been without its costs, and these costs have been borne most clearly by children.

The other main weakness of the liberal approach to the family has been the tendency to talk economics (and individualism) and to neglect family values (and family structure). Conservatives, by contrast, have tended to focus on values but neglect economics. Labour for its part has attempted to do both although avoiding some of the more controversial challenges - as with the gay lobby, or indeed with the implications of tackling family poverty.

Yet the problems being experienced by families today are rooted in economic stress (in terms of both time and money), family disintegration and shifts in values. Any progressive and liberal minded family policy must address both sets of issues simultaneously or it will fail. Moreover, at a time when there is greater public awareness of the full range of costs that society bears when families raise children less effectively than they can, and when the public constituency of support for increased taxes has yet to be built, the liberal agenda needs to take these collective and public interest roles seriously and balance these against the commitment to individualism and free choice. For liberals this also means engaging with the central challenge facing progressive governments in the 21st century - namely how to protect and extend individual freedom in relationships and family life whilst also establishing the nature of family responsibilities.

Now that intimate relationships are forming outside of the married state, this has posed new challenges for policy makers. Like the animals in

Animal Farm, some relationships have historically been deemed more equal than others, and partly as a consequence the state increasingly finds itself drawn into regulating and equalizing rights between cohabitees and the married, between gays and straights, between parents and children, as well as outlining legal responsibilities where none have been explicitly stated. The question of rights and responsibilities has moved inexorably into the foreground.

The diverse nature of contemporary relationships requires that the state intervenes and establishes a clear and principled rights framework for today's extended families. In some cases, this means equalising rights and responsibilities to minimize the hardship that might go with break ups, and the death of a loved one. In other cases, it means extending rights to groups that have historically been denied them - as with gay marriage or with non-resident and unmarried fathers - as the prerequisite for the state's emphasis on responsibilities. As far as possible, the liberal position should be to keep the state out of regulating affairs of the heart as far as possible, with the exceptions of ensuring that couples remain responsible to each other and meet their mutual obligations, and insofar as we need to protect and defend the interests of the child.

These goals will not be arrived at overnight. And they leave unresolved difficult questions for liberals. What role should government play, or what should be its limits, in promoting marriage or tackling divorce? Should liberals have a view about the virtues of marriage over cohabitation? Or should they focus on broader issues of relationship building and the quality of parenting? And what can and should liberals have to say about poverty and its impact on relationships and family life? And finally, is the framework for family rights and responsibilities in need of reform?

In what follows, I set out a framework for equalising rights and responsibilities as the basis for a progressive and liberal family policy and go on to discuss some of the issues which are likely to challenge policy-makers because of the culture of freedom and choice that now shapes relationships and family lives.

Children's rights, parents' rights

At what point can liberals accept the encroachment of the state into family life? The liberal position might be that families today come in all shapes and sizes, and arriving at a clear cut definition of the family is difficult. The 'traditional family' - and by this I mean the male breadwinner/female homemaker and 2.4 children - is increasingly a minority form and far too limiting a definition to be meaningful. Taken to the other extreme, we all live in families whether we are young or old, single or in relationships.

For policy-makers, the simplest solution is to go back to first principles and to state that where there are children, there are families, whether they are intact families or disrupted families, and that the state has an interest in their healthy upbringing. Enshrining children's rights is therefore a vital part of this equation.

Rising rates of relationship breakdown, and the breaking of the connection between marriage and parenthood have increased the financial burden on the state and has led the state into enforcing parental obligations. There is a Liberal Democrat proposal to repeal the Child Support Act and hand decisions back to the courts to be dealt with on a more ad hoc basis. However, whatever the shortcomings of the present Act, there does need to be systematic protection of children and their financial needs in a world of increasingly flexible relationships.

In seeking to enforce parental obligations, pressure has also developed to equalise parental rights - especially when it comes to non-resident parents, the vast majority of whom are fathers. In particular, this has meant extending rights to fathers in ways that are historically unprecedented. For liberals the increased emphasis on parental financial responsibility has to be matched with a parallel framework for rights.

But there are other policy issues which have no obvious answer - including the rights to adopt children as a single parent, or indeed as part of a gay couple. Moreover, the advent of the Internet and the internationalisation of adoption, with even the buying of babies being facilitated, takes it beyond the scope of regulation by any one state.

The rights and responsibilities of cohabitees

The advent of long term and committed cohabitation has posed new challenges for policy-makers. In particular, protection is needed for a cohabitee's rights in the event of death, occupational injury, separation and so on. The key in this instance is to minimize the penalties against cohabiting couples and reform the law to give cohabitees, who are to all intents and purposes living in committed marriage-like relationships, similar rights and responsibilities to married couples - whilst safeguarding their freedoms and choice by allowing them to opt out of these provisions should they not wish to benefit from the same kinds of protection and rights afforded to married couples. An alternative is to introduce a central civil register - building on the civil register currently introduced in London for same sex couples - to allow cohabitees who consider themselves to be in long term and committed relationships to enshrine those commitments legally. The Civil Registration Bill being considered by Parliament would achieve much the same thing nationally. For liberals the challenge will be to ensure that individuals do not have rights and obligations imposed on them should they not wish them. My personal preference is for cohabitees to be in a position to opt out from marriage-like rights and responsibilities, rather than the opting in afforded by civil registration, on the basis that it will afford protection to the most vulnerable whilst safeguarding individual freedoms through the opt out clause.

The gay right to marry

Marriage too should be for all - same sex marriage should be legalised. At the moment, no party has dared to adopt this as a policy, although the Liberal Democrats have gone further than the others in backing the civil registration process outlined above, just as they were at the forefront of the campaign for a common age of consent. A liberal view might be that the more choice we have for individuals the better, and that civil registration could easily co-exist alongside extending marriage rights to this group. But the option needs to be there. There appears to be no public interest arguments against same sex marriage and if marriage is seen to be the prime generator of social capital, trust and attachments in our society, it follows that policy-makers should be concerned to include all couples regardless of sexual orientation.

The rights of the extended family

Families in the 21st century are increasingly extended families both because of greater longevity, which means that four generation families are increasingly the norm, and because of the high incidence of relationship breakdown. The increased emphasis on maintaining ties between parents and children means that the rights and obligations of today's families are increasingly complex.

Issues of grandparents' rights - to see their grandchildren and to be involved in their lives - as well as other inter-generational challenges are moving into the foreground. This may become more marked as demographic change takes effect with an increasing number in the generation of grandparents living longer, more active lives, while the relative number in the generation of parents shrinks. Moreover, parental responsibility could once easily be defined and enshrined through blood ties, but with blended and disrupted families the situation has become far more complex. The emergence of families of choice also begs a rather obvious question: who has the right to draw boundaries between blood and non-blood family members? Is it time that we gave families the right to define their own family obligations, and introduced some kind of family register? Or are there limits to the extent to which people can personalise and individualise their relationships?

For liberals the principle might be that as far as possible the state should not intervene in private relations between adults, but should concern itself mainly with minimizing harm and disadvantage in the event of break up and/or death, and in ensuring that parental responsibilities to their children are clearly enshrined in law.

Enabling choice - liberal family values

Liberals value freedom and choice - indeed the idea of the liberal family is founded on these principles. But freedom and choice cannot always be realised amongst those less fortunate. A certain level of economic freedom is required if people are to be enabled fully to exercise choice. Hence, for liberals any framework of rights and responsibilities needs to take seriously the fact that rights are meaningless without economic support and a framework for enabling choice. This also means recognizing that some of the biggest challenges facing policy-makers in formulating a progressive family policy which supports more, but intervenes less, is to find a way of strengthening the economic base of family life, especially those living in poverty or facing other forms of social exclusion.

For liberals the tone that is struck in debates about the family is also critical. There should be less emphasis on coercion and moral exhortation and more on culture change, on shifting mentalities and mind-sets; less emphasis on what government can do and more on what it can enable others to achieve. At the same time, a renewed and responsible liberalism needs to recognize that families are also generators of public health and social capital. It is inside families that we learn to trust, that we learn to form secure attachments between individuals, that we learn how to be intimate with others whilst at the same time protecting each other's boundaries, that we learn independence in the context of interdependence. Once we recognize that stable families are the bedrock of stable communities, we can begin to frame social policy with the goals of strengthening and preserving families.

There are four main policy areas that liberals should focus on.

1. Strengthening families:

Given the worryingly high break-up rate, strengthening intact families will be essential. For liberals this is not so much about reinforcing traditional families but about recognising that families need to be encouraged and enabled to stay together where they feasibly can. It is about building stronger and more resilient relationships rather than preserving family structures at all costs.

If the goal is to strengthen intact families, the emphasis should be on ensuring that working families benefit from high quality subsidised child care, from paid parental leave, and from a family friendly tax and benefits system. Government will need to shift the balance of financial responsibility away from individual parents to tax payers and employers in recognition of the fact that individual parents have paid too high a price in recent decades. For liberals this means building a public constituency of support for tax increases to finance this.

Welfare to work strategies will also need to be combined with policies which tackle the care challenges for these families, like paid parental leave and child care facilities. In areas of poverty, where the numbers of people forming and maintaining intact families are in most serious decline, targeted welfare to work policies will be a vital means of giving individuals the economic stability to think about family formation.

It will also be important that welfare reform is framed with adults' needs in mind. Just as working parents should be able to benefit from genuine choices between high quality child care and parental leave, so too unemployed parents should benefit from equally child friendly welfare reform. Welfare to work strategies should be supported by a parental care credit for single parent mothers (or indeed fathers), driven by notions of equity and choice, and by public awareness of the importance of parent involvement in the early years of a child's life. All policies should be evaluated by means of a child audit, which assesses the impact of policies on children.

For liberals, involving and enhancing the role of father's in family life will be critical, not just as providers, but as nurturers. As boys continue to under-perform in schools, attention here, and in countries like America and Germany, is already turning to the causes of male under-achievement and to the impact of a father's absence on boys growing up today. Whilst a paid parental leave will be one step in the right direction, we should also anticipate the establishment of a fatherhood task-force in an effort to raise public awareness about father's nurturing responsibilities. (There are highly innovative task-forces and fatherhood commissions in American states, which for instance use sports heroes as role models of fully involved fathers). The task-force's remit should be to review and audit family policy across the board to evaluate how the policies and bureaucratic cultures are father-friendly.

A full involvement of fathers in their children's lives requires expanded notions of child support. The key difference with the current government will be the extent to which these services are grounded at the community level. Typically women have been the 'gatekeepers' to family life and, because they have frequently had negative experiences with these men, they are reluctant to allow them back into their lives. However, the American experience suggests that it is possible to forge a new consensus. Innovative (and experimental) 'team parenting' initiatives have achieved some degree of success in involving fathers and mothers as stakeholders in their children's future and could be replicated in Britain.

Effort should be focussed on low income non-resident fathers, with targeted welfare to work schemes, and personal and social skills training alongside. Initial evidence from various innovative schemes in American states suggest that such programmes have wide appeal both for their employment and educational component particularly when voluntary - provisional results also suggest that schemes which mandate participation are less effective. For liberals it will be vital to strike the right balance between rights and responsibilities.

Liberals are not exempt from the need to shift their own gender assumptions and cultures, and bring fathers explicitly into the family equation in unprecedented ways. The whole direction of family policy, which has historically marginalised fathers and really addressed the mother/child dyad, will have to be re-framed. The emphasis will be as much on shifting gender cultures within the bureaucracies and culture at large, as on programmes and policies.

Recent policy reform has been based on the view that whilst marriage may no longer be for life, parenthood is, and that so far as possible, children should not suffer from their parents' mistakes. This emphasis on parental responsibility and managing the 'good break up' is a pragmatic response to the new realities and it needs to continue.

For liberals, it is vital to start with families as they really are, rather than how we wish them to be, and family policies should not become concerned with competing ways of living. From the perspective of safeguarding child well-being, resources spent on facilitating healthy divorce (and break-ups for cohabiting couples) will be as vital as resources spent on marriage preparation courses. Policy-makers should focus on identifying effective ways of resolving unsatisfactory relationships as well as maintaining healthy attachments between parents and the child, regardless of the relationship between the adults.

2.   *Relationship building:*

For many politicians and policy-makers, public policy should be focused on tackling the fallout of our divorce culture. For liberals this means focussing on strengthening the relationships that people form, and enabling them to deal with the challenges across the life-cycle, while avoiding any facile culture of blame.

Just as tomorrow's adults need the skills and competencies required to cope in the increasingly flexible, competitive globalised economy, so too they need a new set of interpersonal and communication skills to cope with more demanding and fluid personal relationships. The challenge will be to create opportunities to learn - rather than programmes focussed on coercion or moral exhortation, which have been proven not to work. Agencies, such as Relate, providing advice and information, classroom education, soap opera wisdom, counselling and psychotherapy will all play their part. Moreover, moral judgements about one way of life over another will also need to be avoided.

Investment in relationship and parenting skills together will pay off, given that the single most important determinant of successful child rearing is the lack of conflict between parents. We will also need to concentrate our energies on making relationships easier, not on making divorce harder. The divorce process itself offers an opportunity for learning from failure, so that next time around we have the skills to cope. The emphasis will be on self-reliance with government and civil society creating an enabling culture and pathways to learning and advice.

Care will need to be taken in how such information is presented. On the one hand, we need to educate people about the consequences of poor parenting, and in that explain why divorce is the last solution rather than the first. On the other, we do not want to reinforce anxieties and perpetuate dysfunctional behaviour.

The liberal instinct to respect freedom in making and breaking relationships must be balanced with a recognition that private failures in relationships and family life have become a matter of public concern, and are generating direct and indirect costs, which as taxpayers we all bear. We all have a collective responsibility to enhance our capacities to sustain stable and intimate relationships, and government has a role in engendering the conditions for successful relationship building, without interfering in our intimate private lives.

3.   The marriage partnership:

The third major goal should be to foster a marriage culture, given that the two parent married couple remains the most stable unit for rearing children that we have, generating trust, a sense of belonging and the strong and secure attachments required to nurture healthy individuals. A progressive and liberal centred family policy should promote marriage on these terms, although this does not negate the validity of the reverse argument, namely that divorce for couples in unhappy, conflict prone marriages can also be better for all individuals concerned. Given the strong reasons for under-pinning stable relationships, the right to marry should, as argued above, additionally be extended to gay couples.

Education and empowerment are key elements in the support of marriages, and the challenge will be to equip people culturally for a new style of marriage and its advantages. This culture shift should be promoted through education in schools, by financing community based relationship and parenting services, and indeed through voluntary marriage preparation. Individuals should also be encouraged to think through the virtues of pre-nuptial agreements (for money and goods as in France and in America).

This is an ambitious programme of cultural change for liberals, and it will mean discussing the principles underpinning marriage in the 21st century. For whereas marriage in the 20th century is still defined by the concept of romantic love, 21st century marriage should be defined by the concept of partnership, with the implicit assumption that marriages require the cultivation of 'emotional intelligence', work and commitment to sustain them.

Thankfully there is now a body of evidence and understanding among marriage experts about the ingredients and qualities that combine to produce lasting relationships. (There is now a body of knowledge about the dynamics of successful marriages, everything from character compatibility assessments right through to tips on the stress life-cycles of marriages). The idea of 'smart marriage' tools which could be applied by individuals will be a less intrusive way in which the state can enable individual couples to become aware of the pitfalls and challenges that they are likely to face.

Liberal principles of freedom, autonomy, choice and self-expression should also be built into and enshrined in the marriage ceremony. The ceremony is, after all, emblematic of marriage's social function because the ritual of marriage is about articulating a future, about making a commitment, to love, nurture and protect one another. Individuals should also be encouraged to write their own vows, to personalise their own ceremony, and to take responsibility for creating their own future. In keeping with recent reforms over the last few years, the rules and procedures for marriage in this country should, so far as possible, facilitate a more authentic marriage experience. The marriage ceremony should be the first vow of many - it should become commonplace for couples to reaffirm, renew and renegotiate their marriage vows on the basis that even the best relationships need to be worked at.

In the 21st century, the pre-nuptial contract might become the cultural norm, playing the role that betrothal rituals played in pre-industrial society. At all points in the process, the emphasis should be on open and honest communication, since it is this more than anything else which ensures stability and success in marriages. Marriage mentors - volunteers from the community whose mission is to act as a source of advice, support and a reference point for services - should also be commonplace.

What role does or should government money play in engendering a marriage culture? And how far should other groups that do not conform be financially penalised because of this? Why should an unmarried couple in their twenties pay a subsidy to a married couple of the same age, as with the married couples tax allowance? The public health benefits of successful marriages are clear. But the opposite is true for those that are not working. Hence, we should avoid propping up unhealthy marriages at all costs. Similarly, we should also recognize that the role of the state should be to build resilient and committed relationships in general, and this will mean making available to cohabiting couples the same kinds of services that are available to married couples, since it is both audiences that governments must reach if they are really to foster a marriage culture.

4.   Parenting pains:

Although the liberal position might be that it is inappropriate to involve itself in making judgements between child-free couples and those with children, the big picture suggests declining birth rates is a policy concern. After all, we face the prospect of declining birth rates at a time when society is ageing and at a time when the state is looking to the family to bear some of the care responsibilities that goes with this. This raises the spectre not only of inter-generational imbalances but the prospect that there will be insufficient workers to finance the care needs of the elderly. Reversing this trend will require a major cultural shift towards a more child friendly culture, and for many it will involve some form of public subsidy to ease some of the financial burdens that individual parents bear.

Over the last few decades the costs of family life have been shared unequally by individual parents (and by women). Taxpayers and governments now need to share the burden in recognition of the fact that, whilst families raise children, society as a whole typically benefits from their nurture. Paid parental leave for both parents is one of the few policy tools with a proven track record in helping to reverse declining birth rates. Here we should look not to America, where leave is unpaid, but to Europe. Scandinavia has seen a dramatic upturn in fertility since the 1980s as a result of generous paid parental leave. Single parents in particular should be targeted for special supports, with funding for community based 'team' parenting initiatives. Policy-makers should be 'adding on' parenting skills to other measures, such as welfare to work.

The focus should also be on shifting gender and work cultures. Involving fathers will be critical. Government should aim to bring about a healthier, more sustainable balance between work and family life. This will involve a genuine commitment to integrating work and family life. At the same time we will need to avoid differentiating between workers with families and those without; an unhealthy tension between the two can be set up, and the much needed shift in working styles and practices in the mainstream culture will not be achieved.

But a progressive and child centred strategy should go way beyond this. In the end, our policies should focus on fostering a child friendly culture: radically affecting the design of our public spaces, our communities and our workplaces. We need to engender a whole new ethos in parenting. This involves recognising that parents are the primary educators for their children and can play a vital role in enhancing their mental capacities. The early years are particularly important for children's healthy development. The Families and Work Institute, along with the Reiner Foundation in the USA, ran an influential campaign showcasing the implications of the latest research on child brain development. In the future, debates will increasingly focus on the cultivation of competencies in parenting as a cost-effective and efficient means of saving the state money in the long run, as well as creating a virtuous circle of positive personal development, high achievement, and greater well-being.

Conclusion

Liberal policy-makers face a particularly modern dilemma: as we enter the age of the liberal family - where individuals can increasingly opt for families of choice, rather than families of obligation - the state's role is to intervene less and to support more. Yet before the state can intervene less, it must first set clear boundaries around family rights and responsibilities. The fluidity of contemporary relationships and family networks necessitates a clear legal definition of rights and responsibilities to ensure that freedom and choice can be exercised effectively. Equity must be the guiding principle for this legal framework.

But there is an even more fundamental challenge facing liberals. How can they match the rhetoric of families of choice with the reality in some of the poorest areas of Britain? At the moment, the patterns of family formation emerging in these areas are far from being freely chosen, and are the consequence of poverty, failure in education and lack of opportunity. If policy-makers are to enable individuals to exercise genuine freedom to form relationships out of choice, rather than necessity, they will need to build public support for increased taxation and public expenditure to tackle the underlying causes of child poverty and the inter-generational transmission of family instability. Creating the economic conditions for genuine families of choice whilst actively promoting a culture of commitment - inside and outside of marriage - among family members is a challenge indeed, and one which liberals must rise to if families are to live freely and responsibly.

Jo Bamforth assisted in the research for this paper.

---

[1] Source: Office for National Statistics; General Register Office for Scotland; Northern Ireland Statistics and Research Agency, cited in 'Social Trends 31', National Statistics (2001)

[2] 'Marriage, divorce and adoption statistics, 1999' Series FM2 no. 27, Office for National Statistics (2001)

[3] Source: Government Actuary's Department; Office for National Statistics, cited in 'Social Trends 31' National Statistics (2001)

[4] Ermisch J 'Pre-marital Cohabitation, Childbearing and the Creation of One Parent Families', Working Paper 95-17, ESRC Research Centre on Micro-Social Change; 9, 3-4 (1995)

[5] ibid

[6] 'Social Trends 31'

[7] 'Population Trends 105' Office for National Statistics (2001)

[8] ibid

[9] Source: Census, Labour Force Survey, Office for National Statistics, cited in 'Social Trends 31' National Statistics (2001)

[10] Source: Department of the Environment, Transport and the Regions; National Assembly for Wales, cited in 'Social Trends 31', National Statistics (2001)

[11] Dormor D 'The relationship revolution: cohabitation, marriage and divorce in contemporary Europe' One Plus One, London, 1992

[12] For shifts in values see: Inglehart R 'The silent revolution: changing values and

political styles among Western publics', Princeton University Press, Princeton, 1977, and 'Culture shift in advanced industrial society', Princeton University Press, 1990; also Wilkinson H 'The Proposal: Giving marriage back to the people', Demos, London, 1997; Wilkinson H and Mulgan G 'Freedom's Children: work, relationships and politics for 18-34 year olds in Britain today', Demos, London, 1995

[13] Wilkinson H and Mulgan G, 'Freedom's Children: work, relationships and politics for 18-34 year olds in Britain today', Demos, London, 1995

[14] ibid See also Wilkinson H (ed) 'Family Business', Demos, London, 2000 and Wilmott M 'The Millennial Family', Future Foundation, London, 2000

[15] Lewis J, Clark D, and Morgan D 'Whom God hath joined together', Routledge, London, 1992

[16] See Wilkinson and Mulgan 'Freedom's Children', pp. 66-68

[17] Ringen S 'The Family in question', Demos, London, 1998

[18] 'Drop the dead duvet?' MORI/On-line telephone poll, 1998

[19] Health Statistics Quarterly, Autumn 2001, Office for National Statistics

[20] Stanton GT 'Only a piece of paper? The unquestionable benefits of lifelong marriage', Research Report, Public Policy Division, Focus on the Family, Colorado Springs, 1995. Cited in Maley B 'Wedlock and well-being' Centre for Independent Studies, Sydney, 1996

Work
The Social Reconstruction of Life: A Liberal Perspective

Lord Ralf Dahrendorf

The realm of freedom

In the third volume of his *Capital* - thus not in one of the idealistic writings of the young man - Karl Marx wrote a remarkable passage about his old subject, work. He begins with the discussion of 'surplus work' which is the part of the workers' efforts that goes to the capitalist. However, in the capitalist system this does not simply mean more time at work, but more intensive work, higher productivity. Still, it is work: 'The realm of freedom begins only where work which is determined by need and external purposes, ends; it lies in the nature of things beyond the sphere of material production.' All humans have to work to survive, and with rising wants and needs more effort is needed. The best that can be achieved in this sphere is rational regulation. 'But it will forever remain a realm of necessity. Beyond it begins that development of human effort which has its purpose within itself, the true realm of freedom which, however, can blossom only on that realm of necessity as its foundation.'[1]

The passage ends with the laconic sentence which comes almost as a shock after the high language of the rest: 'Shortening the working day is the main condition.' Despite the somewhat involved language, Marx's basic idea is clear enough. The world of work is forever a realm of necessity. It may be organised in a humane manner but it remains a domain of what has to be done, of constraint. Capitalism makes it possible to increase the output achieved by work, and thus labour productivity, enormously. In the end less work creates more output, so that working time can be reduced without 'production' (as Marx puts it in the language of his time) and eventually the gross domestic product suffering. Thus, the 'true realm of freedom' opens up. People gain time (to quote the young Marx of the *German Ideology*) in order to 'do this today, that tomorrow, hunt in the morning, fish in the afternoons, breed cattle in the evening, and criticise after dinner wherever I feel like it, without ever becoming a hunter, a cattle breeder or a critic'.[2]

These are figures of thought which have remained current to the present day; they have become generally accepted. Work must be, for all sorts of reasons - to earn a living, to keep the economy going in order to finance public services by taxation, to gain a social identity. But what must be is only a part of life; the other part of what may or can be, becomes increasingly important. After work, free time, leisure and pleasure begin. Thus we have proceeded step by step from the work society to the leisure society and further to the fun society. The realm of freedom has conquered the realm of necessity.

This at any rate is the applied Marx who dominates the prevailing experience and language of the capitalist world. However, I shall argue in this paper that much is wrong with these notions however plausible they may seem. The work society has not only been reduced but undermined by recent developments. The knowledge society which many think has taken its place turns out to be a society of the deliberate exclusion of many from the modern world of work. Behind such trends lies a paradox which is as yet barely understood; wage labour and capital are no longer inseparably joined but instead capital can grow without the work of the many. As a result work is separated from output and instead becomes an instrument of social control and thus of power. The restraint on liberty in the realm of necessity is extraneous to the act of work itself.

And the solution of such riddles? There are approaches to an answer in the work of Hannah Arendt, and of Robert Heilbroner, though these remain unsatisfactory. A satisfactory answer has to abandon Marx's distinction of the two realms. Freedom is indivisible; either it rules in all spheres of human activity or it is threatened in all.

When the work society runs out of work

This calls for a considerable programme of analysis and is central to our understanding of the politics of liberty in what Anthony Giddens calls a 'runaway world'.[3] Where do we start? 'Shortening the working day is the main condition.' If there is any Marxian vision which has become reality in the century after the publication of *Capital*, it is this. Few remember today how revolutionary the demand for the 48-hour-week and the eight-hour working day once were. The shrinking of working time, of the working day, the working week, the working year and the working life has reached dramatic levels.

There is plenty of research on this subject. some of it summarised in the 'Millennium Paper' on *Future Work and Lifestyles*.[4] Two comments on any generalised summary are, however, necessary. The first is that such generalisations do not apply everywhere. They certainly do not apply in developing countries; but there are important differences within the developed world too. Britain differs from continental Europe, and Japan shows a different pattern again. The United States is still to a much greater extent a work society than the rest of the OECD world. This leads to a second comment. Nowhere in this analysis do I assume developments can lead in only one direction. There is no historical necessity to which we are delivered without chance of defence. It is always possible that things will take a very different turn from the one which they took in the last century.

So far as these developments are concerned, however, there can be no doubt the dramatic changes affecting people's working lives, the working years, the working days, and the conditions of work and employment:

- So far as the <u>working life</u> is concerned a considerable extension of life expectancy has gone hand in hand with an equally considerable shortening of working life. Greater educational opportunities mean that many enter working life later, on average at little less than 20 years of age. At the same time, the institution of retirement has frequently been supplemented by early retirement; in many countries no more (and often less) than 50% of the 55-64 year olds are in employment, with numbers rapidly declining towards zero in older age groups. If one adds the disabled, generously defined as they are in many countries, and others not in employment, the average working life lasts about 35 years while life expectancy is well above 70 years.

- The <u>working year</u> has got progressively shorter owing to a number of developments. The five day week means that most people do not work on 104 days of the year. Public holidays add another dozen or more days to the number. Legal or contractual holiday entitlements have for many reached almost 30 days. One or two attacks of flu or other illnesses have almost become a statutory part of the normal working year. Thus employment takes up little more than half the days of the year.

• Working days (and working weeks) have been shortened too. This is particularly relevant wherever work begins early and is not distributed over the whole day but concentrated in a limited number of hours.

Thus the realm of necessity - if that is the right name - has been massively reduced. As such, this generalisation applies, to be sure, to a minority only. Still the conclusion is worth pondering that work in employment determines only half the lifetime of people, and in this period half the year and again half their waking hours.

Also, one has to add to this picture changes in the circumstances of employment. 'Normal employment conditions' (as Meinhard Miegel calls them), that is contracts for full-time employment and indefinite periods, are still the most frequent type of employment, but already today more than half the working population have different kinds of contract.[5] Part-time work, self-employment, limited-term employment, semi-voluntary unemployment and mixtures of these different conditions (for which people, particularly women, have developed an astonishing imagination) increasingly determine reality.

What remains then of the realm of necessity? Hannah Arendt was the first to speak of a 'work society' which is 'running out of work'.[6] Since then, many others have taken up the phrase, all the way to Jeremy Rifkin's influential book, *The End of Work*.[7] (I am not entirely innocent in this story for as early as 1982 I gave a lecture entitled *When the Work Society Runs Out of Work*.) The proposition behind such analyses is, in a sense, the continuation of Marx's analysis of productivity increases coupled with the shortening of the working day. If one extrapolates such trends further, they suggest that in the end with the help of technology the work of most people becomes nearly superfluous for the creation of the wealth of nations.

The thesis has never found favour with economists. They have mocked the notion of the end of work partly by rightly insisting that there will always be enough to do, and partly out of concern for their fine theories of growth, inflation and employment. I would accept the criticism of economists today insofar as the thesis of the end of work may lead one astray. Even when normal employment conditions become a minority phenomenon there will be enough scope for human activity. In the widest sense of the concept we are therefore not running out of work. However, the work society is reaching its limits. The quantity and quality of the work that is available no longer suffice to structure societies. As a result work loses the ability to structure individual lives. It is no longer realistic to assume that preparation for work, employment, recreation for further work, and retirement as the well-deserved reward for a lifetime of work are the elements from which our lives are constructed. As a result, social institutions change their character and their significance.

Such changes begin with specific matters of concern to economists as well. Even measuring productivity as labour productivity increasingly loses its meaning, especially since it may well happen that in future precisely those simple service jobs are needed which hardly permit increases in productivity, whereas the productivity of the highly technical production of consumer goods increases to even higher levels than today. Our tax systems are still based on the central role of income tax although this is decreasingly relevant. It will be hard to maintain in the medium term that the central source of productivity increases, capital, is not taxed to a significant extent if we want to have a public infrastructure which serves work and leisure in equal measure.

Further socio-economic consequences of the end of the work society are no less dramatic. Education must be more than preparation for employment; it must enable people to live complex lives with long periods of self-responsibility. Free time during the working life requires a readiness and the ability to develop personal initiative. Or do we want to leave it wholly to electronic media and travel agencies? The great subject of the twenty, thirty years after (often early) retirement from working life is a concern which does not just involve those affected. Even unemployment changes its nature. It is after all itself a product of the work society; social historians like Alexander Keyssar have shown how it came about alongside the separation of workplaces - the factories - from the rest of life.[8] What exactly does unemployment mean once the work society loses its defining force?

This is not the only open question. It is a fact that we do not have any real idea what gives structure to individual lives and to communities once employment in normal conditions no longer does the trick.

The knowledge society, or meritocracy

There are a few answers to this question though only partly satisfactory ones. The thesis is often heard at the beginning of the 21st century that we are moving from the work society which has predominated since the industrial revolution towards a knowledge society. Meinhard Miegel has developed this thesis with the caution of the social economist; Anglo-Saxon authors are rather less cautious. Manuel Castells, for example, regards the new economy of information as the solution of all classical problems of classes and their struggles, of inequality more generally, and indeed of power. The information economy is the basis of the 'network society' in which the loops of knowledge generation, rather than the power of people, determine both social structures and the identity of the self. Thus information is the new productive force, and as such it is not an instrument for application but the source of ever new information.[9]

Anthony Giddens shares this optimistic assessment of globalisation unreservedly. 'Marx thought that the working class would bury capitalism, but as it has turned out, capitalism has buried the working class.'[10] The universal chance offered by information has taken the place of the old classes. 'Information and knowledge have now become media of production, displacing many kinds of manual work.' Giddens says this in a conversation with the more cautious economist Will Hutton who does not altogether believe in the great leap forward. He is, therefore, not seduced by Giddens' praise of the 'new economy': 'Famously, the book value of the assets of Microsoft is tiny compared with the trading value of the company as a whole.' Infamously, it did not take long for the 'is' in this happy science to be replaced by a 'was'.

The next step in praising the knowledge society is unsurprisingly an insistence on the importance of education. Institutions of training and education are obviously central for strengthening information as a productive force. In this context the notion of 'meritocracy' has, at least in Britain, gained currency and became for many a goal to be achieved. New Labour advocates of meritocracy have once again overlooked history, in this case the book by their Old Labour colleague, Michael Young, first published in 1958 and entitled *The Rise of Meritocracy.*[11] Young's book was a dystopia, a negative utopia like those of Orwell or Huxley. It describes, from the imagined perspective of the year 2003, a fictitious development towards the meritocracy of those who combine talent and effort. The meritocrats replace the aristocrats and the gerontocrats, the powerful by birth and by age, and everything seems fine until the irritating discovery is made that by no means all are aboard SS Meritocracy, and worse still, that not everything can be accomplished by meritocratic means. 'People are after all remarkable not for the equality but for the inequality of their talents.' As a result, two classes soon emerge below the meritocrats. Young speaks of 'corps' like army units. One is the 'Pioneer Corps' which consists of those who cannot quite reach the meritocratic heights. They perform the manual tasks which require certain skills and are above all indispensable. Then there are those who cannot even make the Pioneer Corps. They form a 'Home Help Corps' for those highly personal services which no-one wants to touch any more and which are yet necessary to keep social life going.

Young pursues this new class society through its increasing rigidity to the eventual revolution. It is worth reading the whole book rather than just repeating unthinkingly its pleasant sounding title. Adair Turner, the very practical economist, has no aversion to the knowledge society or even meritocracy, but nor does he have exaggerated expectations. He distinguishes rather between the new 'high-tech' and the old 'high-touch' economy, thus the high technology of the world of information and those good old services which will forever be hands-on, like changing a light bulb or looking after elderly relatives. 'So the new economy is not just high-tech or knowledge-based. It is a mixture of the high-tech and the high-touch, the thin air and the physical, the knowledge-based and the plain old mundane jobs that need to be done.'[12] Nor is it, Turner adds, all that new.

On closer inspection the knowledge society does not fill the vacuum of anomie which the disintegrating work society leaves behind. To be sure, activities emerge which rely to an increasing extent on knowledge, or at any rate on the use of information. The resulting jobs frequently defy our generalisations about shortening the working day. The meritocratic masters of the knowledge society work long hours, six or seven days a week, without many holidays, though only for a few years, that is until their knowledge and their energy decline. For the others who live in the high-touch world, work presents above all the problem that it does not give them the satisfaction (or the monetary rewards) which they seek. Thus, it is an open question whether the knowledge society can be an effective successor to the work society, and it is certain that if it takes the shape of meritocracy it will lead to new tensions which do little to advance the life chances of the greatest number.

Capital only

Adair Turner's book, from which I have just quoted, is entitled, *Just Capital*. It is a political economy of liberty or, as the author himself puts it in the subtitle, a book on 'the liberal economy'. By that Turner does not mean the neo-liberal economy of pure capitalism. Rather, it is one of his core theses that there is much more room for variations of capitalism than the naive theory of globalisation permits. Economic actors do not have to follow the American, or even a single European model in order to hold their own in global markets. National policies too have more options than the believers in inescapable global constraints like to admit. Here, as elsewhere, liberty means diversity.

The title of Turner's book, *Just Capital*, is deliberately ambiguous. Capitalism and justice are not incompatible; this is one meaning. However, the other one is that only capital is left as a dynamic force. Let me pursue this idea a little further, and in my own, not in Turner's language. The idea that capital and labour belong inseparably together has accompanied all theories of capitalism from Adam Smith and Karl Marx to John Maynard Keynes and beyond. Adam Smith has shown in some detail how the improvement of the circumstances of all requires an alliance of capital formation and productive work. Unproductive work (which actually sounds similar to Turner's 'high-touch' work) may be socially useful but does not lead to growing wealth. Marx describes the same phenomenon in polemical language: 'The existence of a class which has nothing but its capacity to work is a necessary condition of capital'.[13] Capital, however, is itself a condition of the ability of workers to live. Keynes raises all this to the macro-level and seeks ways to secure full employment by the visible hand of the state, because without full employment dangerous destabilisation threatens. On account of such theories Keynes has been called the saviour of capitalism.

For 'high-tech' capitalism in an age of globalisation all this is no longer so true. Even full employment loses its old meaning. While one-third of those who are employable in the technical sense are not formally employed, they could not be accurately described as unemployed in the old terminology. Even the unemployed find all kinds of alternatives, from the clever use of state support through moonlighting to family work. While politicians still use the language of the old work society they can no longer win elections with it. For the 'high-tech' economy and its growth the majority of those of working age are not needed as employees.

This does not mean that they could live entirely beyond the labour market. For one thing the global class which found its wealth on the crest of new technological waves needs all kinds of helpers and servants. Some of these, like the army of IT managers in almost all institutions, may even be described as productively employed. Many others, however, are there to provide comfort if not pleasure: the driver, the domestic servants, the captain of the private yacht with his crew, the golf professional. Then there are the many in the 'Pioneer Corps' and, above all, the 'Home Help Corps'. They range from security personnel to carers for the old, from plumbers and gardeners to kindergarten teachers and nurses.

The so-called service economy has long become a misleading description. It includes a 'high-tech' part and a 'high-touch' part. Banks and insurance companies belong to the former, personal services to the latter. For economic growth only the former are needed. In this sphere, capital has become independent; labour, wage labour at that, is needed to a decreasing extent. On the other hand, in the hands-on world, work has become independent; fixed capital, even machines play only a limited role. This means that for the future of capitalism a large part of work - and of workers - has become dispensable. Capital without labour is conceivable, indeed nearly real in many places. Conversely, the same is true for labour without capital.

It may be convenient to have such labour without capital, but we can live without it. In principle, the 'Home Help Corps' is dispensable. In many places there no longer are domestic servants (except perhaps as near-slaves, such as illegal immigrants without papers). In the United States, people like to have their pizzas delivered at home, their cars washed and their shoes cleaned; in much of Europe most people go out and get their pizzas themselves, while on the way home driving through an automatic car wash, and what happens to their shoes remains invisible. Even European do-it-yourself markets provide a part of the explanation of the lower employment ratio compared to the USA.

Thus a peculiar separation of wage labour and capital has taken place. It is simply no longer true that the existence of a class which has nothing but its capacity to work is a necessary precondition of capital. The advocates of the knowledge society offer an explanation of the often mysterious multiplication of capital: in the new 'informational economy', argues Manuel Castells, a 'virtuous circle' drives progress. 'The products of new information technology industries are information-processing devices or information processing itself.'[14] This is moreover a 'cumulative feedback loop'. In other words, knowledge breeds knowledge breeds knowledge ad infinitum. I am not sure that I can easily visualise such processes, but it is evident that the networks which drive them forward are very different from the old, almost fatal connection of capital and labour.

It has to be reiterated, however, that this is at best half the story. Capital without labour means labour without capital as well. As a result, work in a society transfixed by information and technology falls back to more primitive forms, not just of activity but of dependence, than were present in advanced industrial society. Information capitalism creates a divided world.

Work as social control

As we try to bring such generalisations and abstractions back to reality, two sets of facts strike the eye. One is that the world of work has itself assumed the patchwork pattern which has characterised this analysis. The old world of work with its clear structures - training, work and leisure, retirement - is a mere memory for most, though the memory lingers. This is as significant for the motives of young people as it is for the tax system and for social structures. For the time being, Manuel Castells's network society is a figment of the academic imagination. Meinhard Miegel comes closer to reality with his cheeky suggestion that most people (he actually said 'most Germans') want nothing as much as a permanent job, yet once they have got it they make every effort to reduce the work which it demands.

The other striking reality is that work has assumed an increasingly peculiar role in public and political discourse. Companies gleefully announce that they are going to create 400 jobs in North Wales or Normandy as if this was the objective of their enterprise. (When a few years later jobs, and sometimes services with them, are destroyed in order to raise profits, they make less noise about it.) Politicians insist with suspicious emphasis on their intention to find work for everybody. This is particularly the case among those advocating the 'third way' who keep on stressing the central role of work. In his most recent book Anthony Giddens actually uses the 'employment rate' as a measure of the success of 'new social democracy'. The argument underlying such claims is that of the necessary balance of rights and duties. Giddens calls it the 'supreme motto of the new politics' that there are 'no rights without responsibilities'.[15]

The thesis may seem plausible, but it is also dangerous and certainly illiberal. There are rights, and there are duties or responsibilities. The citizen has both. But both stand on their own. Freedom of speech must not be made dependent on paying taxes, and the right to vote not on the readiness to help neighbours. This is why a policy is destructive of liberty which insists that the unemployed should get no support unless they are actively seeking work, and even more that the disabled or young mothers should have no claim to state support if they do not work.

Anthony Giddens is well aware of the changes in the world of work; he speaks himself (if in inverted commas) of a world 'beyond the work society'. However, New Labour (and the continental advocates of the 'New Centre') are obsessed with the necessity of work. Work for them is the first civic duty. If one listens carefully to their pronouncements, one discovers, however, that work in the sense of employment is no longer valued as a source of income, of social identity or of economic growth, but as an instrument of social control. Only when all are in employment does it remain possible to hold society together and thus control it.

The notion is not altogether incomprehensible. Young men without work have become one of the most threatening features of modern society. They are susceptible to many kinds of fundamentalism, all the way to beliefs which make the martyr's death seem desirable. Everywhere young men are responsible for the majority of those irritating trespasses and petty crimes which give rise to the demand for a rigid notion of law and order. There can be no doubt that it would be a good thing if these young men had something sensible and meaningful to do. But this is the point: it has to be something they regard as making sense and having meaning. Work as a measure of control, forced work, does not solve the problem of the footloose young men. Not even conscription - where it still exists - has this effect.

Not only those in power are concerned about the work society slipping away. After the weakening of the family, the local community, the church, employment relations were the last structures to give people support. Yet it would be a strange perversion of the thesis with which I began this paper if the realm of necessity was to be used as a weapon for deliberately restricting the realm of freedom. Compulsory work is like all compulsion a step away from liberty. We should never forget the cynicism of the slogan above the gate of Nazi death camps which said, *Arbeit macht frei*, 'work makes free'.

The true realm of freedom

Whoever has followed my observations, analyses and doubts up to this point will wonder where the journey is going to end. The journey is one of ideas, but ideas about the way in which real people in the real world construct their lives. Moreover the end is clear; its name is freedom. But what freedom? And how can we achieve it?

Plausible as Marx's distinctions may seem at first sight, I have been critical of the separation of the two 'realms' notably because it implies an intrinsically and, therefore, hopelessly unfree realm of work. The rise and fall of the work society offers us different chances. Many authors have tried to define these. Three writers are worth discussing because even their errors point the way to an answer. All three have written, as I have here, about the work society which is running out of work.

Hannah Arendt has been mentioned already. She starts her analysis with the distinction of three kinds of human activity which she calls, 'labour', 'work' and 'action'.[16] Labour secures our survival; work creates products which endure; action, notably political action in Hannah Arendt's understanding, 'creates the conditions for a continuity of generations, for memory and thus for history'.

The definitions make it clear that Hannah Arendt assumes a hierarchy of activities. In that respect she follows Aristotle, though she interprets his *vita activa* more extensively, and, rather surprisingly, turns to the *vita contemplativa* only at the very end of her book on *The Human Condition*. However, while Aristotle implies a class structure in his distinction - the slaves have to work so that the free can devote their lives to contemplation - Hannah Arendt sees, in the last two centuries, an increasing liberation of all from labour and work. This means that people find the space for the *vita activa*, for civic activity in the political community. They can concentrate on shaping public affairs.

In this way Marx's distinction remains essentially intact. This is also true for Ulrich Beck whose argument follows the facts of social development more closely than Arendt's. Beck emphasises the 'invasion of the discontinuous, the flaky and informal into the remaining bastions of the full employment society'.[17] This development is in many ways precarious but it makes it possible 'to discover the growing wealth of time in the growing lack of paid work'. He continues, 'The antithesis to the work society is the strengthening of the political society of individuals, the active civil society in local communities.' There emerges alongside employed work what Beck likes to call 'citizens' work' as 'an alternative source of activity and identity'.

In effect Beck combines Karl Marx and Hannah Arendt. He retains the distinction between the realms but regards the growing 'flakiness' of one as the chance of the other - the realm of freedom - for public, political activity. This extraordinary place of the political is perhaps above all a German aspiration. (It runs like a thread through Jürgen Habermas's ethical discourse.) It must remain an open question what this can really mean for ordinary citizens. In our context the point, however, is that Beck too seeks freedom in a new and different realm, and in any case beyond the work society.

The third author who is relevant here is the political, or perhaps the philosophical, economist Robert Heilbroner. He takes a different line. In an unusually subtle little paper (originally a lecture) he considers *The Act of Work*.[18] Capitalism has replaced the brutal dependence of the workers as serfs by the labour contract which is concluded in a labour market encompassing the whole of society. This was not the 'perfect' or 'natural' liberty stipulated by Adam Smith; the need to find employment still meant dependence and 'surplus labour'. At the same time, however, capitalism set in motion a process which increasingly reduced the dependence of the workers and thereby changed their motives. They were now working to prove themselves, to be successful. This may evoke 'the tantalising vision of a world without work', but another prospect is more realistic: 'not a society without striving and effort, but a society without submissive striving, without subordinative effort'. 'A world without work is a fantasy, and a dangerous fantasy at that.' However, a world without domination and subordination is imaginable. 'Can work, the first and perhaps most basic form of social subordination, become the first and perhaps most emancipatory form of social responsibility?'

Even in Heilbroner's analysis traces of the theses of Arendt and Beck are recognisable. Self-determined, responsible people who shape a society that strengthens their full potential are Heilbroner's vision too. But in one crucial respect his approach is different. We can find answers only, he says, 'by struggling to achieve whatever freedom is possible within work - not from work'.

It may be that the dissolving work society was only a temporary hope. Time and again the reminder is needed that there is no necessary progress in history. But it may just be the case that new opportunities for the construction of human lives have emerged which make it possible for some examples of freedom to become real. In this connection I like the concept of activity. Freedom is life as activity - that is, as autonomous, self-determined action. Such activity does not begin in our leisure time or otherwise beyond work, but in work itself. Thus what we call work, that is jobs and employment, becomes a part of a continuous process of activity which includes educational experiences and the association with others for various purposes as well as hobbies and leisure pursuits (though these expressions stem from an era which had lost the unity of activity in our lives).

Life as activity: this is not an empty ideal. In a sense it means regaining earlier forms of life at an enormously enhanced level of wealth and without the often brutal past forms of dependence. It may well be that women find it easier than men to construct their lives as one activity in a variety of dimensions. But there is no shortage of examples even of young men who combine vocational training with sport and playing in a band and friendships and even a little politics, and all that in freedom. Thus the end of the work society is not the end of work, and certainly not the end of activity, but, if it is to become the beginning of a society of activity in freedom, we cannot afford to sit back and wait. It requires our untiring effort.

---

[1] Marx K 'Capital', Vol. III, ch 48/III

[2] Marx K 'German Ideology', Introduction, A/1

[3] Giddens A 'Runaway World', Profile Books, London, 1999

[4] Age Concern 'Millennium Paper - Future Work and Lifestyles', London, 1998

[5] Kommission für Zukunftsfragen (Meinhard Miegel) 'Erwerbstätigkeit und Arbeitslosigkeit', Part 1, Bonn, 1996

[6] Arendt H 'The Human Condition', Doubleday, New York, 1959, ch. III/16

[7] Rifkin J 'The End of Work', Putnam's, New York, 1995

[8] Keyssar A 'Out of Work', CUP, Cambridge, 1986

[9] Castells M 'The Rise of the Network Society', Blackwell, Oxford, 1996

[10] Hutton W and Giddens A (eds.) 'On the Edge', Jonathan Cape, London, 2000, p. 22 seq

[11] Young M 'The Rise of Meritocracy', Thames & Hudson, London, 1958. See particularly p. 92

[12] Turner A 'Just Capital', Macmillan, London, 2000, ch 2

[13] Marx K 'Lohnarbeit und Kapital', Reclam, Leipzig, 1925

[14] Castells M op cit

[15] Giddens A 'Where now for New Labour?', Polity, Cambridge, 2002. See pp. 11, 79

[16] Arendt H op cit

[17] See Beck U 'Die Zukunft von Arbeit und Demokratie', Suhrkamp, Frankfurt, 2000. By the same author 'Schöne neue Arbeitswelt', Campus, Frankfurt/New York, 2000

[18] Heilbromer R L 'The Act of Work', Library of Congress, Washington DC, 1985. See p. 22 seq

Retirement

Frank Field MP

There are five themes highlighted in this chapter:

- what retirement income is;
- why retirement issues are heading up the political agenda;
- the possibility of raising the retirement age;
- the 'best' way to fund a pension;
- the Pensions Reform Group (chaired by the author)

The funding of retirement is the aspect of it with which public policy should be most concerned at this time. There are certainly important issues of health, recreation, and so on, but all these require funds. Indeed the concept of retirement, of not having to work as much for a living (or indeed at all), implies the provision of financial resources for that lifestyle. So how an income from a source other than paid work is secured is where the main political interest in retirement should be located.

There is no panacea for securing this income. The most common way of funding retirement is a pension, which is a claim on future resources. The state pensions of most people reading this will, at least in part, be a claim on the income of people who have not yet been born. An occupational or personal pension is usually funded and thereby involves withdrawals from the capital market. This, therefore, also diminishes the resources available to the working population.

There is a balance to be struck by politicians when trying to ensure that pension promises will actually be honoured. Push too far in favour of the retired population and workers will revolt and vice-versa. More concrete examples of this will be offered later. For now, my second theme is why retirement issues are heading up the political agenda.

It has been said of this government, fairly or unfairly, that they only believe something if it is in the media. One of the media's favourite hobby-horses is that we have an ageing population. This is certainly true. There will be about a 50 per cent rise in the number of people over 60 over the next generation.[1] Fertility rates are also low by historic standards. The next twenty years will see the baby-boomers reaching retirement and this country will have a demographic profile very markedly different to any point in its history.

Elsewhere the imminent change is even more dramatic. Indeed the more one looks at other countries the clearer it becomes that the UK, along with the US, Holland and Denmark is in a rather good position. Germany has a very substantial state pension, currently worth 67 per cent of average earnings; recent reforms - against which there have been vociferous protests - have succeeded in reducing this to 65 per cent. In Britain the state pension is worth 15 per cent of average earnings and falling. Moreover the working papers for the World Bank's Commission on Global Ageing included calculations showing that official estimates in Germany and Japan have not been accurate on the full scale of the future financial burden.[2] Official projections in Japan, for example, very considerably underestimate likely future life expectancy and in consequence is over optimistic about projected dependency ratios.[3]

So there are serious fiscal problems for some of our European and non-European partners. Pension commitments have been made that cannot be met, yet there is no political will to take on the very powerful interests supporting those unsustainable commitments. On top of this, health and caring expenditure will grow massively. For some the final bill seems too painful to contemplate. Governments may have to borrow and thereby weaken the growth prospects of their countries. With the introduction of the euro this will not be a decision left to individual states.

However, demographic change only tells us one part of the story. Changing expectations are another part of the plot. More and more people have an expectation of a leisurely retirement. This expectation is, I guess, in part a result of the early retirement packages on offer to some employees over the past fifteen or so years.

But unfortunately it is simply not possible for ever greater numbers of people to enjoy an early, well-funded retirement. Indeed, I would be surprised if the period of early retirement did not come to be seen as an anomaly resulting from a specific coincidence of events including large pension fund surpluses, and the downsizing of companies adjusting to structural changes in industry. Early retirement will always be an option for the wealthy few, but its history to date is best seen as part of a tacit deal by employers and government to buy off opposition to redundancies at a time when surpluses in pension funds fortuitously allowed them to do so. This view is supported by the fact that so many less well paid workers, usually employed in manufacturing firms that were wiped out in the 1980-81 recession, were subsequently thrown onto incapacity benefit - where they all too often stayed until reaching the retirement age. This form of early retirement is rather less glamorous than the stereotypical image of Spanish holiday villas and other little diversions, but it is early retirement nonetheless.

In any case the key point is that from the mid-1980s onwards voters began to see the *option* of a well-funded early retirement as the norm. But, as I have mentioned, the factors that made this possible were transient.

Subsequent legislation has also helped bring to an end the expansion of early retirement. Nigel Lawson, as Chancellor of the Exchequer, introduced accounting rules limiting the surpluses in pension funds to 105 per cent of liabilities. This move has never been adequately explained. It led to the apportionment of excess surpluses amongst scheme members - a process that continues to cause deep controversy. It also meant that the trend of large surpluses being used to fund early retirement for ever greater numbers of employees was arrested. Occupational pension schemes are not as well positioned as they would have been had Lawson's change to their accounting rules not been enacted.

The monumental achievements of David Lloyd George in paving the way for the welfare state are well known. The life expectancy for males when Lloyd George introduced the first state pension was 48 years of age. The pension was payable at age 70. Leaving aside the effect of infant mortality, the fact remains that in Lloyd George's day many more people than now worked a full life without reaching the retirement age.

When in 1995 the then Secretary of State for Social Security, Peter Lilley, equalised the retirement age for men and women, it was a legitimate response to a very changed labour market. Lilley sensibly equalised the age prospectively with the measure not taking full effect until 2020. However, it should be put on record that omitting to increase the retirement age for everyone to 67 has now been recognized as an important opportunity lost.

Raising the retirement age would allow a more generous basic state pension. Perhaps it would also allow other schemes to follow suit and hopefully offer somewhat more generous pensions. With the Government trying to put half of school leavers into higher education and more people hoping for a long retirement, sooner or later the claims on income will be challenged.

But if we are to retire later and work longer then there is a need for a very considerable cultural change both by older workers and by their employers and colleagues. The Commission on Global Ageing is expected to make useful recommendations in its *Report to World Leaders* in March 2002. These include the ending of a seniority based payroll, and the opening up of new opportunities to older workers. My guess is that most people will come to support such moves but the transition from our seniority based workplace hierarchies to a system where older workers move to different jobs and remain motivated to welcome new challenges will not be easy. Much will depend on successfully extending healthy life expectancy as well as overall life expectancy.

The key area of concern remains the 'best' way to fund a pension. Towards the end of my period as Minister for Welfare Reform in 1998 I was asked by the Prime Minister to produce a paper on what course pensions reform should take. In opposition I had presented him with a copy of pension proposals costed by the Government Actuary. The approach, which aimed at universal pension coverage, but not in a state-run scheme was to be the basis, if not the blueprint, of discussion in Government about how best to beat pensioner poverty.[4]

A review of pension policy had been running in the Department of Social Security since the election. Its basic idea was to extend personal pensions. My draft paper for an alternative strategy was, I later learned, never read by the Prime Minister. Another agenda was being pursued in the Treasury and the then Department of Social Security (now rebranded as the Department of Work and Pensions). The outcome was revealed in December 1998 with the publication of the Green Paper *Partnership in Pensions.*

The strategy was now tripartite; first, there was to be a new form of personal pension, trading off some control over investment with lower charges, aimed at those with modest incomes between £10,000 and £20,000 per annum. For those below this level there was to be a new version of SERPS called the State Second Pension. Today's poor pensioners were to be offered greater help through a more generous level of income support, the Minimum Income Guarantee.

It was immediately apparent therefore that, although the government was acting with the best of motives, it had in fact ducked radical reform. Each of these three reforms was a development of existing arrangements. None of them promised a new settlement that would as far as possible guarantee a good retirement income for all. Moreover, the Government's short-term strategy to help today's pensioners was designed in a way that would discourage long-term saving.

Soon after resigning I brought together the Pensions Reform Group (PRG) to propose long-term reforms that would stand a real chance of defeating pensioner poverty and allowing people on modest incomes to know throughout their working lives that each penny saved would be additional wealth in retirement, not savings to be counted against means tested benefits. Such a reform would simplify massively the savings terrain for savers, employers, regulators and government.

Membership of the PRG is broad based. All three major political parties are represented, along with the pensions industry, the broader financial community, the voluntary sector, and academe.[5] The formation of this group saw the first time that MPs from three main parties have come together with a wide ranging group of interests to address the problem of pension reform in the long term.

The proposals the PRG have put forward keep the pay-as-you-go basic state pension - and build on top of it with a compulsory funded element. There are valid arguments that can be put forward in favour of both pay-as-you-go and funding. Pay-as-you-go avoids stock market risk and issues of management and governance. Funding on the other hand arguably generates a more secure claim on wealth as it is based on something akin to property rights. Funding also allows for investment globally giving scope for the better returns and more favourable demographic structures that might be available there. There is, of course, much more to this issue than can be sketched out here but it seems to the Pension Reform Group that there is a powerful case for a hybrid scheme which spreads risk and can take advantage of both methods of funding.

The core proposal of the PRG is best thought of as a company pension scheme for whole nation. We have called it the Universal Protected Pension. It can be summarised as follows: a compulsory funded scheme on top of the basic state pension for all workers coming into the labour market. Our initial proposals involve an additional employee National Insurance contribution of about 5 per cent. There would be no additional costs for employers. Included in the scheme would be all those in work, and all those with legitimate caring responsibilities. The current costings do not allow for the inclusion of the unemployed and the incapacitated, although, if the welfare regimes for these groups were further developed to ensure both that claimants were doing all they could to find work and that those claiming incapacity benefits were genuine cases, then it might be possible to include these groups too.

As things stand the basic state pension in forty years time will be worth about 10 per cent of average earnings.[6] In today's money this is about £50 per week. Our reform aims to add a funded tier to this to achieve just under 30 per cent of average earnings - or about £150 in today's money.

Before a reform this ambitious came into effect there would, of course, be a great debate about what level the funded component should aim for. The level I am talking about is by no means a fortune. However, two crucial points should be made. The first is that the PRG and, I believe, any serious commentator involved in the UK pensions debate, does not consider it the job of state to provide a high standard of living for all in retirement. Individuals have to be free to make those savings choices, and redistribution on that scale would not be viable in any case. What we think is the concern of the state is the provision of a level of income that is above means tested benefit levels. Our proposed level of income is well above the Minimum Income Guarantee (£92.15 per week) and, according to the Government, well above the total level of means tested benefits for the vast majority of pensioners, with the exceptions perhaps being a small number of pensioners claiming housing benefit for properties with extraordinarily high costs.

This has some very important implications. First and foremost, every pensioner retiring from a working life will retire free of poverty - the primary aim of the Group's work. Second, every worker will know that every penny saved throughout a working life is a penny gained in retirement. At present, low earners who save know that they are doing so instead of receiving benefits. Naturally this creates perverse incentives. Very few pensioners will be caught in means tests. Freedom will be widened for the low paid and income will be increased. Similarly, employers will know that the provision they make will not be instead of benefits. With the Universal Protected Pension there will be no moral hazard. The reform goes with the grain of human nature to provide for oneself and one's family.

A further significant advantage flowing from each worker retiring with this level of income is that even if they spend their additional savings they will not be 'falling back on the state'. Many of you will recognize this argument immediately as the classic justification for annuities. Our reform will mean that the requirement to annuitise defined contribution pension savings could be abolished at no cost or risk to the Treasury.

As the pension came into payment the state would disengage from the generous means tested benefits currently paid. These benefits would still be available, but they would be paid to very many fewer people. Figures from the government suggest that the savings would run up to £10bn per year or more in today's money.[7]

To sum up, the Pension Reform Group wish to put Britain's pensions on a sustainable footing. Our view is that this is best done through a hybrid part-pay-as-you-go and part-funded scheme delivering a pension well above the means tested benefits level. The gains from such a proposal are many. Our ideas are now undergoing critical examination and improvement by leading figures from all walks of life. We hope to build a consensus based on a pension that ends poverty in retirement.

Ben Forsyth, secretary of the Pensions Reform Group and a researcher working for Frank Field, assisted in the writing of this paper.

---

[1] Government Actuary's Department, 2000-based Population Projections for the United Kingdom

[2] Shieber S and Hewitt PS 'Demographic Risk in Industrial Societies, an analysis for the Commission on Global Ageing', *World Economics,* 2000

[3] ibid. p. 3

[4] Field F 'How to Pay for the Future', Institute of Community Studies, London 1996.

[5] Membership of the Pensions Reform Group: from the three major political parties Howard Flight (Shadow Paymaster-General), Steve Webb (Liberal Democrat spokesman on Social Security), and Frank Field; from the pensions industry Tom Ross, Alison O'Connell, and Lord Vinson or Roddam Dene (who with Phillip Chappel originated personal pensions); from the broader financial community Simon Linnett of Rothschilds, Peter Gray, formerly of the Chartered Insurance Institute (now of Hertford College, Oxford), Matthew Owen of Morgan Stanley, Kate Barker, formerly of the CBI (now of the Monetary Policy Committee); from the voluntary sector Carolyn Hayman, Chief Executive of the Foyer Federation; from academe Alan Deacon, Professor of Social Policy at the University of Leeds. The group's secretary is Frank Field's Research Assistant Ben Forsyth.

[6] Hansard, 5 February 2001, column 365W.

[7] Figures obtained in answers to Parliamentary Questions.

Dying

Harry Cayton

Dying is the ultimate private activity. Yet it is surrounded by public meaning. Death through terrorism, death in a train crash, the deaths of children, the deaths of celebrities all attract our attention. Death, that most solitary, intimate event is overseen by medical, communal, cultural, religious and legal rules and regulations.

It is almost impossible to sneak away from this life unnoticed; even the anonymous victim must be found a name, even the pauper given a grave. The state regulates death as carefully as it does life. You need a certificate, you have to have a reason. Until quite recently while the state was content to kill you, you were forbidden by law to kill yourself.

In this essay I want to discuss the ways in which the public and private aspects of death are increasingly in tension. Autonomy, individualism and choice have become key ethical and social values. Religions have ceased to provide a coherent world picture which society as a whole can share. Medical science has transformed life expectancy and created a whole new class of the very old.

It is impossible to write about the process of dying without writing about the event of death. How we anticipate and experience dying is dependent to a great extent on how we understand death and what meaning we attach to it.

Recently I was struck by the terrible reality of a photograph in a national newspaper[1]. It was a photograph of a dying man; an Afghan fighter shot in the chest. He was pictured half kneeling, his face uplifted to the sun, his eyes closing. Blood poured from the wound in this chest and from his mouth, crimson against his dark beard and dusty robes. He was supported on either side by a comrade, their faces turned towards him were in shadow. They bore him up as he coughed his life away. In the background seated soldiers looked on impassively.

Perhaps it was the chiaroscuro in this photograph, perhaps it was the brutal honesty of its focus on death, but it seemed like a Baroque painting of a dying martyr flanked by saints or bishops. It could be one of those slightly sickening, lurid pieces which hang in the side chapel of an Italian church, in which the saint looks heavenwards bearing the instrument of their own death: St Catherine with her wheel or St Sebastian with his arrow, an icon for the faithful to learn from, providing both intimacy and distance. But what struck me also was the photograph's caption. This dying man had a name, not a full name I'm sure, but the caption read, 'Northern Alliance soldier, Amin, who was shot in the chest, takes his final breaths…'. Suddenly he was a person not a photograph and the impact of the public and private was all too real.

But this was in a secular newspaper not a church. My icon was without context, or rather the context was one which attached no meaning to Amin's death, one which invited me to share in this private moment of a complete stranger but offered me no help in understanding it.

It is often suggested that the modern generation is protected from death. I do not think that this is the case. It is true that children who grew up, as I did, in the 1950s and 60s did not experience the death of family or friends as early or as frequently as did our parent's generation. I was well into my tens before either grandparents or a friend died, whereas both my parents lost siblings from scarlet fever or tuberculosis, and of course many friends in war.

As a generation we have not had to fight a war, but war and death have not gone away. Indeed modern media give us a grandstand view, bringing death into our living rooms, live from the scene. Motorway pile-ups, plane crashes, the murder of a teacher or pupil at a school gate; we are not protected from death. Perhaps even, as Kate Berridge suggests in her recent book 'Vigor Mortis'[2], we have outed death and are making it fashionable.

Last century two world wars each transformed social and political relationships. The Victorians had relished death. They lived alongside it, sentimentalised dying and glorified the dead. Their funerals were elaborate, their mourning rituals complex and lengthy, their cemeteries a wonder of art and science - as anyone who has visited Kensal Green will know.

But the First World War changed that. There were too many dead. The living needed to get on. Those who had died were away from home. It wasn't possible to bring them back to England, and anyway the War Graves Commission did not allow it. Nor did it allow gravestones to represent difference of status or rank. Death, in war at least, became part of government policy with standardised graves and communal memorials throughout our towns and villages, and the national focus was on communal remembrance not individual mourning.

In the Second World War it was the deaths of civilians at home, through bombing, which was new. Death was immediate, present and public. The needs of public health and the practical problem of dealing with so many bodies led to a rapid increase in the number of cremations. The exigencies of war meant that funerals were to be got over with and bereavement could not be allowed to disrupt the war effort. Wives and mothers who previously might have observed long periods of mourning were quickly back at work.

Of course, it is the Holocaust which finally transformed our understanding of death in the 20th century. Institutionalised genocide of the Jews in Europe and the mass killing of Japanese civilians at Hiroshima and Nagasaki were both scientific, calculated, dispassionate. Genocide has always been a policy open to tyrants, but the Holocaust's systematic efficiency made murder public policy in a way never seen before. The sheer scale of deaths in Europe during the Second World War and subsequently in Cambodia, Rwanda and the Balkans have desensitised us to individual deaths and made numbers our only measure of horror. Think of the competition in speculation of our news media inflating the number dead in the Ladbroke Grove train crash - over 70 according to one tabloid, and the sense, almost, of disappointment when it turned out to be 'only' thirty-one. We have experienced the same in the speculation about the number who died in the Washington and New York attacks, as though the absolute truth of each individual death was less important than the communal sense of shared horror in the unique scale of the atrocity.

At the end of the First World War the focus was on dignified secular remembrance. After the second, the state encouraged people to look forward not back. Rebuilding Britain, hope not mourning, was the theme, and just as death had come to many through war so in peacetime medicine was to bring new life, dramatically reducing infant mortality, preventing and curing diseases and raising life expectancy. Death seemed to disappear from social life. People died in secret and their dying was not discussed. Children no longer went to funerals, which anyway were quick and quiet. Euphemisms abounded, people 'passed away' or 'passed on' or 'passed over'. As medicine extended not only our lives but the process of dying, people stopped dying at home. When they went into hospital or institutional care they moved out of society and became, as it were, invisible. If we went to visit them on Sunday afternoons they were attached to drips and tubes, nurses bustled about with pills and potions. Even the flowers we brought in 'to brighten up the ward' seemed to presage their funeral. Death became not a natural end of life but a medical failure. Medicine's new task was to prevent death or at least delay it as long as possible.

The arrival of AIDS was a great awakening for my generation. Forgotten, private death crashed back triumphantly into the public domain. Remember those fantastic government advertisements? Great looming tombstones symbolising doom and destruction but completely failing to mention safe sex. AIDS also reinforced the medicalisation of dying; it gave new energy and focus to professional care of the dying and it shocked us in that (initially at least) it was young people who were dying, many of them from the glamorous worlds of theatre, music and fashion.

The medicalisation of dying has, of course, brought many benefits - pain relief in particular and certainly great improvements in the control of symptoms and the promotion of well-being. At its best, palliative care creates choices and gives dying people emotional, social and physical reassurance and support in the context of what Cecily Saunders has called 'the vulnerable friendship of the heart'[3].

Medicalisation of dying has also brought about invasive treatments, the undermining of autonomy, the over-use of drugs and the apparent domination of length of life over quality of life. It has made many people fearful that at the end they will receive medical treatment but not care.

Although a majority of people express the wish to die at home, the medicalisation of dying means that their wish is rarely granted. Recently, a young man dying with MS had to go to court to demand that he be allowed to move out of a local authority institution to die at home. 50 per cent of people died at home in 1950. Now only 26 per cent do (2000). The older you get, not least for reasons of prolonged frailty, the less likely you are to die at home.

The medicalisation of dying might be seen as appropriate if medicine were only concerned with the physical. But medicine has always existed in a cultural, ethical and religious framework. It has always been about relieving suffering as well as preventing death. Indeed many healthcare professionals are motivated by altruism and sometimes by deeply held religious beliefs that may be at variance to those held by people they are caring for[4].

The disappearance of a shared religious, specifically Christian, context for dying and for understanding death has added greatly to the public private tension over care of the dying, and in particular the ethics of end of life decisions such as the withholding and withdrawal of treatment and the legalisation of euthanasia.

I am not suggesting that we live in a secular society, far from it. What we seem to have is belief without theology, and religion without doctrine. At one end of the scale, we have pick and mix religion, incoherent and inconsistent, at the other, religions fragment into sects and factions.

Rather than promote secularism, public policy actively encourages religion. Communal acts of worship are legally required in schools and current education policy promotes separate faith schools. Christianity is protected by blasphemy laws. Recently, in its proposed measures responding to September 11th, the government attempted to go further and give all religions unique legal protection, despite the fundamental contradictions in what each holds to be true and in their attitudes to ethics and society.

Our society seems to want the security of religion without the thought and the rituals of religion without the effort. Funerals have come to reflect this. Increasingly people privatise the event.

'I felt emotionally inspired by [Princess Diana's] funeral', one wife whose husband died of cancer on the same day said. 'My husband was buried in woodland in a beautiful handmade willow coffin which was borne on green boughs on the back of a farm cart pulled by two shire horses with purple plumes. Apart from that it was very simple with just white lilies. A local Anglican vicar read the 23rd Psalm and a Buddhist priest did a death chant. Everyone agreed it was a vast improvement on the traditional funeral'.[5]

A post-modern funeral indeed

Respect for the body after death is fundamental in all human societies, though how that respect is expressed varies greatly. Nevertheless, I have found myself disquieted by the funeral rites which have followed the Alder Hay Hospital organ retention scandal. The contempt for the parents' wishes and the disregard for their dead children shown by the practices in that hospital were deeply offensive. The name Pity 2 which the parents' action group has adopted stands for 'Parents Interring Their Young Twice'. The focus is on the original burial of an incomplete body and the repetition, in some cases for several body parts, of further funerals. The parents have obtained a change in the regulations relating to cremations to enable further cremations of parts of the same body.

I find these repeated funerals difficult to comprehend theologically; they apparently give more importance to the body than to the soul. Yet they are supported, perhaps out of compassion rather than conviction, by the churches in ministering to these families. Our funeral rites have become disconnected from religious orthodoxies.

The rituals these parents are performing, like all funerals, strive to give meaning to the suffering of the living and mark an end to the suffering of the dead. But suffering, whether of the dying or of those they leave behind, is a challenge for all the world religions.

Dr Michael Stroobant, Director of Palliative Care at Les Deux Alices Hospital in Brussels, responding in the Catholic Sentinel to Diane Pretty's attempt to obtain legal consent for assisted suicide, said, 'Death always involves suffering regardless of the quality of care and of those who give it. One must accept the suffering because death is part of the mystery of life'[6].

This puts the Christian point of view; if suffering is not actually intended by God it is nevertheless part of His plan and to be embraced as a prelude to Heavenly release. This is clearly a comfort to those who believe it, but I for one would not wish my pain control to be in the hands of a doctor who believed that suffering was inevitable.

From a Jewish perspective, Dr Ezekiel Emanuel, in an editorial in the British Medical Journal, seems to take a different view[7]. He says 'the process of dying is less than optimal' (I don't think I'll argue with that), and that 'dying is a painful process filled with *unnecessary* suffering' [my italics]. He sees the anticipation of suffering as the fuel for campaigns in favour of euthanasia and argues that what is needed is 'time, resources and energy' focused on the care of the dying. This would, he believes, end calls for euthanasia. I'm not sure I find this argument either morally or practically satisfactory. We should indeed put time, energy and resources into the care of the dying but with the intention of improving the well-being of dying people not in order to reduce the grounds for euthanasia. Indeed, I think Dr Emanuel misses a significant part of the argument. Those who seek the legislation of euthanasia do so not because they want more treatment but because they want less; or rather they wish to retain choice and control, and dignity. The medicalisation of dying - and the high profile cases of Persistent Vegetative State (PVS) around which public debate often focuses - leads people to believe that medical practice may go beyond the desirable in sustaining life regardless of its quality.

This was the focus of conflict around Ann Winterton MP's Private Members Bill on Medical Treatment (Prevention of Euthanasia) in 1999. The Bill arose ostensibly from concern about the improper use of 'Do Not Resuscitate' orders in hospitals. Certainly there was some evidence that decisions were being made, without consultation or consent, that the quality of life of some dying patients was so poor that they should not receive active treatment in the event of, say, a cardiac arrest. The real concern here seems to me not to be the withholding of treatment but doing so without consultation or consent and often without regard to the feelings or wishes of relatives.

It is well established care practice that treatment of the dying should not be futile or burdensome. The Winterton Bill went well beyond these issues. If it had been passed it would have redefined medical treatment so that the giving of sustenance and maintenance of life by artificial means would have become standard practice, thus extending life for many in a burdensome and futile way and completely denying them choice or autonomy.

'Most would accept', the BMA Ethics Committee has written[8], 'that there is no absolute duty to prolong life at all cost since death is an inevitable reality. The point at which treatment becomes excessively burdensome for a patient must be judged on a case by case basis'.

Decisions about the withholding and withdrawing of treatments are perhaps the most common dilemmas facing healthcare workers for the dying. Their difficulty has been increased by the ability of health technologies to keep people alive even longer and in ever more dependent a state. This is sometimes portrayed as argument between quality of life and length of life but this is not really the case. The problem is that medical technology is now capable of prolonging poor quality of life.

The debate about whether the giving of sustenance by tube is good care when its sole purpose is to maintain life, and when there is no hope of recovery, has been the subject of important legal consideration. The arguments have been well set out in the House of Lords decision in Bland[9]. The House of Lords rejected the submission that the removal of the gastric tube necessary to provide feeding to Anthony Bland and the discontinuance of gastric feeding was an act of commission and therefore murder. Since Bland was unable to consent, he could only continue to be lawfully treated if it was in his best interests. The Law Lords argued that, 'Assessment of best interests must take account of pain and suffering which prolonged feeding and medication may cause but also the constant invasions and humiliations to which a patient's inert body would be subjected'.

In the eight years since this case there have been fewer than 30 applications made to the court for a declaration that it is lawful to withdraw artificial sustenance from PVS patients. Decisions to withhold such procedures are being made daily and the General Medical Council has recently issued draft guidance to help doctors, in consultation with other staff, carers and family to make such decisions.[10]

This guidance has been greeted by some as that well known 'thin end of the wedge' or dangerous 'slippery slope'. One barrister, quoted in the *Daily Telegraph,* said that such withdrawal of treatment was 'largely indistinguishable, legally, from the criminal homicides of Dr Shipman save that his method was quicker and pain free'.[11]

This seems to me rather to overstate the case. It certainly shows an ignorance of the unpleasant 'invasions and humiliations' of tube feeding. A recent review of research into nutrition in the terminal stages of life indicates that artificial feeding not only fails to provide benefits but increases risk of infection and does not improve comfort.[12]

There are two kinds of these slippery-slope arguments. One asserts that once a practice is accepted we are logically obliged to accept other practices as well. If we believe, for instance, that it is in a patient's best interests to withdraw artificial feeding we will consequently be committed to active euthanasia. I don't think this holds up. There are significant and rational grounds for distinguishing between the withdrawing and withholding of treatment and the active killing of a patient. The differences are circumstantial, moral and legal. They are readily understood. In saying we accept the former we are not in any way led to accept the latter.

The second slippery-slope argument is from human nature. This is not a moral argument but a psychological one. It asserts that, if we begin to kill people in order to save them from terrible suffering or in response to their considered request, we shall find ourselves killing them for other reasons. This appears to be the argument suggested in the *Daily Telegraph* report referred to above; GMC guidance allows withdrawal of treatment so, in due course, euthanasia will become common practice.

This argument is subject to empirical tests and I don't think the evidence is there. As we know 'Do Not Resuscitate' notices have existed for years. We also know that hard decisions about the withdrawal and withholding of treatments are made daily. Yet there is no evidence of an increase in euthanasia. The guidelines from the BMA and the GMC do no more than clarify best practice. Certainly they do not either encourage or condone euthanasia.

It is not possible to consider dying in the context of public policy without discussing euthanasia. This is especially so at a time when Diane Pretty's attempt to use the Human Rights Act to assert her right to die has been so much in the news and when she is taking her case to the European Court.

The arguments around euthanasia are complex and it is not possible for me to do justice to all of them here. I want to consider a relatively narrow question - whether the medicalisation of dying, our high tech ability to prolong and maintain a life of total physical dependency, combined with the disintegration of religious consensus, mean that public policy in relation to assisted suicide should change?

Diane Pretty's case has made one thing very clear. Euthanasia is illegal in the UK. Her arguments failed under both Article 2 of the Human Rights Act, the right to life, and also Article 3, the right to be free from inhuman and degrading treatment. The argument that the 1961 Suicide Act gave her the right to commit suicide also failed, the Law Lords asserting that the law decriminalising suicide did not imply approval of it and that, therefore, it was not discriminatory that the ability to commit suicide was unevenly distributed. Mrs Pretty remarked 'I feel as though I have no rights'.

It is hard, however, to see what private good comes from Mrs Pretty's existence. She is suffering greatly. Her death is inevitable. She is rational and capable of decision making. To assist her suicide would surely be an act of mercy and a moral good for her as an individual. Her inability to commit suicide is inequitable and therefore unjust.

Only if we approach the problem from a religious perspective; asserting the sanctity of life and that suffering is part of God's plan, can we find good in this situation. We may argue - back to the slippery slope again - that Mrs Pretty's good must be sacrificed for the greater good, that of protecting the old and frail from involuntary euthanasia or protecting society as a whole from moral failure. This is a utilitarian argument which denies her autonomy, dignity or justice.

Different forms of assisted suicide, under different kinds of regulation, are legal in the Netherlands and in the state of Oregon. In the Netherlands, even after 20 years of acceptance, only 3.4 per cent of all deaths are by euthanasia or physician assisted suicide. In Oregon, after three years of legalised 'assisted suicide', the number seeking to end their lives this way remains less than 30 per year, 0.1 per cent of those dying in the state. The reasons given by those seeking assisted suicide are loss of autonomy, loss of bodily functions, and inability to partake of those activities which give life quality. 23 of the 27 were in hospice care, all 27 had health insurance.[13]

These numbers tend to refute the slippery slope argument. There has not been a flood of euthanasia under these jurisdictions. But it also raises for me another question. If the demand for euthanasia is so small, is this private dilemma properly a public issue? Some would argue that it is. The injustice of Diane Pretty's case requires remedy, they would say, however rare its occurrence.

But it is appropriate when thinking of moral issues, particularly in health care systems, to be proportionate in our response. Equitable distribution of resources is inevitably in conflict with unequal need for them. Might it be that the legalisation of assisted suicide or euthanasia would be disproportionate to the problems of dying? Doctors and nurses as professionals express deep unease about the profound change in relationship that might be brought about by legalising euthanasia, though it is not clear that people in the Netherlands are more mistrustful of the medical professions than we are here. It seems that finding the right balance between the private and the public in our response to dying is essential if quality of death is to be achieved.

I should like to propose three approaches that we should pursue to help improve the process of dying and the choices that surround it.

The first is a sustained, resourced and committed drive to improve care of dying people: to encourage home hospice care, make medical technology our servant not our master, to promote choice and autonomy and openness about quality of life as opposed to length of life. The Voluntary Euthanasia Society argues that the legalisation of euthanasia brings about such an improvement by causing individuals, families and medical professionals to focus on care of the dying.[14] This is the reverse of Dr Ezekiel's argument cited above but, similarly, seems to seek the right thing for the wrong reason. We should improve the lives of the dying because that is the right thing to do, not for any other reason. Euthanasia, by extending autonomy and ending suffering, may be part of that improvement but cannot be the cause of it.

Part of improving care of dying people will be cultural and educational change to bring together private and public discussion of death. Children need to be re-engaged with dying, families need to discuss amongst themselves what a good death might mean. We need to help people make choices before they become unable to do so. Of course, this is best practice already, but it remains elusive and inaccessible to all but the few.

My second proposal is the active promotion of advance directives. An advance directive is a clear expression of a person's wishes for medical treatment in the future, should they become incapacitated and unable to consent at the time. Effective use of advance directives can help improve the quality of life of people who are dying and limit the excesses of burdensome treatment. Consent is fundamental to medical treatment. One of the key triggers for those who seek the legalisation of euthanasia is loss of autonomy. Advance directives extend that autonomy into the end of life when capacity may be non-existent or severely impaired. In common law clearly expressed wishes, whether written or spoken, are binding on doctors.[15] A proper framework around advance directives would enable those who wished to have some control over their treatment and quality of life and some power in a situation where they have become powerless. Advance directives would not be able to demand euthanasia as this would remain illegal. Both the Law Commission and the Lord Chancellor's Department[16] have recommended a change in the law to provide a regulatory system for advance directives, but so far the government has been dilatory in its response.

I am aware that anticipatory consent is difficult. Medicine will change, and we may alter our perception of quality of life. But within a regulatory framework advance directives could be valid only if regularly updated and confirmed. There is a risk, but advance directives will be for the few. All medical treatment is a risk. Many people already die under medical care from poor practice, illness caused by treatment, medical accidents or actual disease. Dying too soon rather than too late is a risk people signing advance directives would have to accept, but then we accept that risk every time we enter a hospital.

For my third proposal, I follow the argument of James Rachels, an American philosopher who has written extensively on euthanasia.[17] He considers the historical response of juries and judges to those accused of murder when their defence is diminished responsibility. In practice courts have been sympathetic; defendants have either been acquitted or, if found guilty, been given suspended sentences or probation.

We allow 'self defence' as a justification for murder. My proposal is that 'mercy killing' should also become a legitimate defence. Such a change in the law would place the onus on the defendant to prove his or her case. The burden of proof would transfer from the prosecution to the defence and it would ensure a full consideration of the evidence of benign intent. It would mean that those contemplating such an act would need to do so openly and to have clear evidence of consent. It would mean that in carrying it out proper scrutiny would be required. It would mean that should Mr Pretty accede to his dying wife's wish and assist her suicide he would have grounds for a defence against a charge of murder. And it would end the legal and moral muddle of present judgements, where doctors or relatives are found guilty of murder but released on probation or given a suspended sentence because of 'exceptional circumstances'.

All this is a bit messy. But then, unfortunately, dying is a messy business. Balancing public and private good in a changing society which no longer has shared religious values is never likely to be tidy.

'Call no man happy until he's dead' wrote Aristotle.[18] He meant that happiness could only be judged on the whole balance of a person's life. A good death is part of that balance. A good death is part of a happy life.

In developed countries in the 21st century dying is for many a more extended experience than it has been at any time in the past. We need to enhance the autonomy of people who are dying by improved care and clearer legal frameworks for consent to treatment, including advance directives. We need to acknowledge a minority of cases where voluntary euthanasia or assisted suicide may indeed be a genuine private good and to make wise provision for them.

Medicine is making dying more comfortable but also more protracted. Dying is becoming not a brief prelude to death but a stage of life. We need to live it as such.

---

[1] *The Independent*, 24 November 2001

[2] Berridge K 'Vigor Mortis; the end of the death taboo', London, 2001

[3] Nyatanga B 'Why is it so hard to die?', Dinton, 2001

[4] Neuberger J 'Dying Well; a guide to enabling a good death', Hale, 1999

[5] Quoted in Berridge, 2001, p. 108

[6] Stroobant M, Director of Palliative Care Unit at Les Deux Alices Hospital, Brussels. Quoted in 'Catholic Sentinel', 14 January 2001

[7] Ezekiel E 'Euthanasia: where the Netherlands leads will the world follow?' In *BMJ* 322, 9 June 2001, pp. 1376-1377

[8] BMA 'Withdrawing and withholding treatment', 1998

[9] Lady Justice Butler-Sloss 'Withholding and Withdrawing Life-Prolonging Treatment', Lecture given to the General Medical Council, July 2001

[10] General Medical Council 'Withholding and withdrawing Life-Prolonging Treatments: Good Practice in Decision-making' (draft) July 2001

[11] *Daily Telegraph*, Life Support Guide is 'First Step to Euthanasia', 6 August 2001

[12] Olde Rikkert MGM and Hoefnagels WHL 'Nutrition in the terminal stages of life in nursing-home patients' *Age & Ageing* 30: 436-438, 2001

[13] Voluntary Euthanasia Society, *Briefing*, 2001

[14] op cit

[15] Age Concern Institute of Gerontology, Kings College Centre of Medical Law and Ethics, 'The Living Will; consent to treatment at the end of life', London 1988

[16] Lord Chancellor's Department, 'Who Decides? Making decisions on behalf of mentally incapacitated adults', 1997

[17] Rachels J, 'Euthanasia' in 'Matters of Life and Death' (ed. Regan T), New York, 1979

[18] Aristotle 'Nicomachean Ethics' Book 1

New ideas, new approaches, new solutions

Centre for Reform

The views expressed in this pamphlet are the views of the authors. They are not necessarily shared by individual Trustees, members of the Advisory Board, members of the Management Committee, or the Director. Authors are not necessarily members of the Liberal Democrats, and Centre for Reform pamphlets do not constitute Liberal Democrat policy.